The Soul & The Sea

Essential Healing for Everyday Life

What people are saying about

The Soul & The Sea

This is a book – whose chapters are a series of rooms – written by an outstandingly gifted healer and poet, one who is in touch with her heart and her imagination and who is therefore able to address the deep suffering of people living in our dysfunctional, uncaring, soul-banishing culture. As she says, "I write from the star in my heart; that is what guides me and my creativity. It is as though by following the intensity of my feelings, I open and walk through the doorway of the divine."

I would recommend this wise, caring and inspirational book to men and women who seek a deeper connection to Life, to the Earth, and above all, to their Heart and their Soul.
Anne Baring, PhD (hons), author of *The Dream of the Cosmos: A Quest for the Soul*

This fascinating and heart-warming book, written by an intuitive healer, gifted teacher and Jungian psychologist, takes us on a journey of inner healing. Rich with personal experiences and archetypal influences, we're guided through various rooms of our own psyche under the watchful eye of the Divine Mother. Complete with practical advice and exercises, this is a valuable book in times of individual and global transformation.
Dr Christine R. Page, author of *The Healing Power of the Sacred Woman*

The Soul & The Sea is an inspiring weave of personal narrative with depth psychology and spiritual wisdom traditions. It is also a 'stitching together' of the microcosm of the personal with the macrocosm, as the soul of the world. Benig's work makes for a compelling read, and brings many elusive concepts down to earth, in an accessible and grounded way. It is timeous in that we need such works that can speak to the suffering soul, stripped from the jargon and obfuscations of intellectual and spiritual disciplines, yet grounded in her many years of experience as a healer, writer, activist and educator. In *The Soul & The Sea*, Benig also offers valuable practices such as journaling, dreamwork, active imagination, engagement with the natural world, and practical methods in a unique synthesis distilled from her many years as a healing practitioner.

Mathew Mather, PhD, author of *The Alchemical Mercurius: Esoteric symbol of Jung's life and works*

In our soulless, COVID-ravaged world, beautifully written books on Soul like this one are an enormous blessing. Benig is not only a poet, shaman and mystic, but also a healer, analyst and transpersonal visionary, and thus great wisdom flows through every page. Indeed, she takes the reader deep into the psyche to explore universal human experiences such as the dark night of the soul, and particularly what is required to live an authentic and whole life in these very precarious times.

The second part explores the existence of what Benig calls "healing rooms". One room helps us confront and heal the many wounds in our hearts that prevent our soul life coming into its own; another room, the "birth room" helps women heal traumatic birth experiences, while the "life room" offers us advice as to how to live with grace and integrity.

This important book is not only a must read for all therapists seeking to expand the range of the way they work and see the world, but it is also important for the person in the street in need of guidelines to help them live with greater depth and joy and who wish to make the shift from being part of the problems in the world, to being part of their solution. A tour de force.

Serge Beddington-Behrens, MA (Oxon), PhD, K.O.M.L., Transpersonal Psychotherapist, Spiritual Educator, and author of *Awakening the Universal Heart*

Benig Mauger has written an interesting book, which will speak not only to the professional audience of Jungian psychology, but also and more significantly to the vast non-professional audience suffering the ever increasing dark night of the soul in our perilous age. Written in the style of a memoir and weaving together her experiences as a birth therapist, Jungian psychotherapist and spiritual healer, she escorts us through various healing rooms as a companion, addressing us with a personal appeal to acknowledge the healing power of conscious suffering. If there is a singular quality that animates this book, it would be its emphasis on remembering the necessity for the grieving process in an age so drawn to the continuous enticement of the new and so benumbed by its displays that it has forgotten how to mourn.

Robert D. Romanyshyn, PhD, Prof Emeritus of Clinical Psychology, author of *Victor Frankenstein, the Monster and the Shadows of Technology: The Frankenstein Prophecies*

Also by Benig Mauger

Songs from the Womb: Healing the Wounded Mother
978-1898256540

Reclaiming Father: The Search for Wholeness in Men, Women and
Children
978-0954701208

Love in a Time of Broken Heart: Healing From Within
978-0954701215

The Soul
& The Sea

Essential Healing for Everyday Life

Benig Mauger

BOOKS

Winchester, UK
Washington, USA

JOHN HUNT PUBLISHING

First published by O-Books, 2023
O-Books is an imprint of John Hunt Publishing Ltd., 3 East St., Alresford,
Hampshire SO24 9EE, UK
office@jhpbooks.com
www.johnhuntpublishing.com
www.o-books.com

For distributor details and how to order please visit the 'Ordering' section on our website.

Text copyright: Benig Mauger 2022

ISBN: 978 1 80341 127 9
978 1 80341 155 2 (ebook)
Library of Congress Control Number: 2021953224

A CIP catalogue record for this book is available from the British Library.

Design: Stuart Davies

UK: Printed and bound by CPI Group (UK) Ltd, Croydon, CR0 4YY
Printed in North America by CPI GPS partners

We operate a distinctive and ethical publishing philosophy in
all areas of our business, from our global network of authors to
production and worldwide distribution.

Contents

Dedication
To the Great Mother in the sea and land of my birth
that nurtures my heart
and the Divine Feminine spirits of my
Lineage that illuminate my soul
and to Her Holiness Sai Mai for her eternal love and
for reminding me who I truly am

Acknowledgments

Conceiving and giving birth to this book has been a very different journey for me than that of my previous books. For although the seeds of *The Soul & The Sea* were gestated before the COVID-19 crisis it was only when we entered lockdown in 2020 that I put pen to paper. When I did, the book was written quickly. And so, strange as it may seem to acknowledge a world pandemic in this context, I must do so. It provided the backdrop to a fertile inner process culminating in my being able to access the wisdoms and teachings I have shared in this book.

I'm sure I am not alone – many books were written during lockdown, but for me, the forced 'aloneness' or seclusion functioned not simply to force me inwards but to reinforce the essential greater message of this tumultuous time. Nonetheless, there are many to thank.

To Her Holiness Sai Maa whose Divine Feminine grace and force opened me fully to my spiritual destiny and to my own lineage as a healer, spiritual teacher and initiate, and whose fierce love rooted in me a deep knowing and awakening that has transformed my life and enriched my work as therapist and healer. I offer my deep gratitude and love. To my fellow students on Maa's healing programs over the years as well as my soulmates and fellow travellers walking the earth as flawed but beautiful human souls – thank you.

To my clients and all the men and women who have shared with me both the joys and pains of living and loving. I continue to feel privileged to be part of, and to witness the struggles of all my fellow travellers on this journey that is life. To all those who afforded me the privilege to be present at their births, both physical and spiritual, I thank you from my heart.

To my colleagues and fellow soul pilgrims, especially to Serge Beddington Behrens whose patient listening and generous heart helped unravel the last remaining block and set me on my way. Special thanks to Anne Baring, Christine Page, Robert Romanyshyn, Mathew Maher and Serge Beddington Behrens for reading the manuscript and writing endorsements. To Veronica Lydon, soul sister, friend and healer, whose skill and Feminine wisdom revived a tired body and flagging spirit on my numerous visits. To various wise women and healers whose gifts of insight held the book in spirit whilst it gestated in me.

To the people at Shreyas yoga retreat near Bangalore, India, where the book was seeded. Namaste and thank you. The daily yoga and sacred cocooning of Shreyas enabled the heart healing and psychic opening needed to set me on course. And to my ever bountiful and loving spirit guides especially the Divine Feminine essence of Mary Magdalene, whose presence continues to inform and inspire me. To my first analyst and my first 'nana' who reminded me who I truly am.

To the publication team at John Hunt who believed in my work enough to publish and to all those involved in bringing this book to birth.

To my partner Willie for his unending support and for listening to copious amounts of reading and rereading, and to my loving canine companion Pepa, whose constancy and unconditional love I miss every day.

And finally, I offer eternal gratitude for my deep-rooted connection with the sea and the land around my soul home in Connemara, Ireland.

Introduction

Eight years ago I moved to live in my 'soul' home by the sea in Connemara, Ireland. Having previously lived in big cities with my children whilst maintaining a busy psychotherapy practice, the move was to prove pivotal to my life and work. Being born by the sea in a remote part of Ireland and having a natural affinity to nature and animals, I had always migrated to this part of the world at holiday periods during my long years of city living. In 2013, with my family grown up, I decided to give in to the hunger inside me to experience a more tranquil, natural life so that I could surrender myself to an inner calling. A calling that had grown over the years until I could no longer ignore it. A call of the sea to dive deep into my inner being and connect with the voice of my soul. And although I had grown in my life and been informed by my years and experience as a therapist so that I knew that healing was not simply a matter of will or of the application of good psychotherapeutic knowledge, it wasn't until I answered this call that I understood the mystical nature of transformation and healing. And lived it. This book is the result.

My house borders the sea on the Wild Atlantic Way, and since these shores are always prone to storms, sleeping in my loft room overlooking the ocean, I can always hear it. I am endlessly inspired by and drawn by her vast energy. As a Jungian therapist I know the sea represents many things: a symbol of the mother, the vast unconscious and the ever life-giving Feminine. With my growing and constantly evolving need to experience the spiritual component of life, the sea represents everything connected to the Divine Feminine – the source of eternal nourishment and healing. I had been primed. The same period of time around me making this move to live full time by the sea coincided with a surge in energy towards the more healing aspect of my work and teachings, some of which had evolved as a result of my last book *Love in a Time of Broken Heart: Healing From Within*, published in 2008. I began leading my Healing From Within workshops here at my soul home in the form of three-day retreats facilitating a deeper immersion into soul. Designed to guide participants on an inner journey to wholeness, these experiential workshops incorporated Jungian with developmental psychological themes. Using guided meditation, sacred poetry, art, myth, drama and dreamwork, participants were invited to learn how to heal from within. Intuitively understanding that clients on a retreat would be nurtured by proximity to the sea, it was easy to incorporate free time in nature as an integral part of the workshops.

At the same time, given my remote location, I began to teach online via webinars and online courses. Throughout all this, the sea continued to call me and inform my work. At a deep visceral level I had always understood or rather 'felt' the healing energies in the earth around me, but the sea reached me at a deeper, less defined, more mystical level. She spoke to me, pulling me into experiencing my femininity in a new and endlessly nurturing way. My connection with her enriched my life and awakened, it seemed to me, my own Sacred Feminine nature, long dormant. She brought up the most vulnerable and sensitive parts of me, my deeply emotional nature and my heart wounds. My life as a woman, past hurts and emotional pain to my tenderest female soul and body surfaced through my connection with the sea. I found I developed inner sight and my latent psychic intuitive abilities and intelligence evolved in a natural organic way. With that, although well into middle age, perhaps aided by solitude, I developed a deeper sense of and appreciation of myself as a woman.

As a child I had always been fascinated by the tale of *The Little Mermaid*. And since my family are French (Breton), my earliest bedtime stories were always read to me in French. I still remember making my long suffering auntie, who came to live with us periodically during my earliest years when my family endured the hardships and isolation of being refugees in a strange land, read and reread *La Petite Sirene*. My little girl's heart seemed to beat in tune to some resonance in this tale I felt but didn't yet understand. I lived and relived the pain and sorrow of the Little Mermaid, who loved a mortal and who had to trade her most precious possession, her voice, for human legs, so as to win her Prince's love. The central message was somehow that love was unobtainable, or rather that one had to sacrifice part of oneself in order to be loved. Perhaps a presaging of later heartbreak, I took this story to mean that love was out of reach somehow and that love and heartbreak were inextricably entwined. *The Little Mermaid* is a sad story of impossible love and yet of course there is a great beauty in the search for true love. A search that is universal and part of the human journey, and which I have come to understand as a spiritual longing or hunger for connection with the Divine.

We lived by the sea and as a child the sea was very much part of my life. I remember long summer evenings returning home against a sunset mauve sky, my father's small boat laden with lobsters which we had collected from the fishermen in the nearby island of Inishturk. I can still hear the gentle hum of the outboard motor as we snaked a path home through the oily calmness of the sea. The wonder and beauty of a sea that was benevolent and quiet as it could be angry and perilous still holds a special, enchanted place in my heart. On those summer evenings the sea somehow held us, allowing us to glide across her waters and bask in her care. Sometimes on our way back home, we stopped at one of the small islands, High or Friar Island, and decanted on to the rocks with our kettle and thermos of milk complete with biscuits and sandwiches. My brother and father would start a small fire, the kettle would be placed on it and we would lay out our tea on a napkin or tablecloth my mother would have packed. Waiting for the kettle to boil was magic somehow; the sun low on the horizon, small creatures darting about in the fading light and the sounds of the sea below all combined to create an enchanted world. Not wanting to stray too far, we were allowed to wander about and forage in the rocks until my mother called us back and the tea was made. Occasionally, if we were lucky, we encountered seals on the way home, particularly during warm weather evenings. Grey soft creatures with long whiskers, they seemed to call to us with their big mournful eyes. We knew to keep very still so as not to disturb or frighten them and sang to them gently as my father had taught us. They would lift their heads and stare at us as though in recognition of our shared heritage and history on these western shores and seas. It seemed to me they were communicating somehow, and it still thrills me to see seals when they swim close to the shore beneath my house.

Life moved on, I grew up, studied in Dublin, married, started a family and eventually settled in London, UK. I completed further training in psychoanalytic psychotherapy and started a clinical practice. At the same time, with my training and interest in yoga, holistic health, dance therapy and pre- and perinatal psychology, I had created a Holistic Birth Centre where I held prenatal and post-natal yoga-based preparation for birth classes. Couples came to me to help them prepare for the birth of their babies. The women took part in regular yoga-based stretching and meditation classes which they returned to after birth with their new babies. It was during this time and at the end of my psychotherapy training that my first book *Songs from the Womb* was published. Considered groundbreaking at the time, my book challenged one of the most pervasive myths of our time, namely that birth is purely a physical event to be managed by doctors. Based on my experience as a birth teacher, therapist and mother, and backed by recent research in pre- and perinatal psychology, *Songs from the Womb* placed birth and life in the womb as a formative experience creating patterns we carry with us into later life. Anchoring my insights in Jungian psychology, I highlighted the 'loss of soul' many feel as a result of our modern medicalised way of birth where technology has replaced nature. And for a while in the early 1990s I was a Birth Activist in my area of London, to help women create fulfilling and empowering birth experiences in a largely medicalised birthing culture. Additionally, where giving birth had been traumatic or wounding, my work was designed to help women recover from and heal these experiences either in one-to-one or group therapy. These were inspiring years for me and very much part of my spiritual path. I have often thought that everything I have ever learnt about soul and 'spirit' came from babies. Babies have not long left the spirit world and are as yet, therefore, not too distant from God or the Divine.

Time and tide came and went and I returned to live in my native Ireland in 1995. I set up a clinical practice in Dublin and was heavily involved in teaching and supervising on several psychotherapy trainings. I found working in Ireland to be very different to the UK. There was not yet an established culture of therapy or counselling in Ireland at that time. Nonetheless, psychotherapy trainings were sprouting up and teachers with experience and good training were in demand. I had no difficulty finding work, and enjoyed being back and working in my native country. My book *Songs from the Womb*, groundbreaking at the time, was well regarded and I set about writing another. This time my focus was on the role of the Father, the masculine complement to the Mother and the Feminine. *Reclaiming Father* was published in 2004. With its subtitle *The Search for Wholeness in Men, Women and Children* it was not difficult to see that perhaps at an as yet subconscious level, my focus was on the Sacred Inner Marriage. *Reclaiming Father* struck a chord at a time when it appeared the rights of (unmarried) fathers to their children were limited or non-existent; my book put fathers on the map as it were. In a time of increasing divorce rates, when men's traditional roles were being questioned and a growing number of children were being raised without fathers, *Reclaiming Father* examined his role in early life. In addition, it answered such pivotal questions as: How does a man's father influence how he himself becomes a father? How can our experience of being fathered affect how we relate to an intimate partner? The publicity generated by my book on Fathers served to highlight my work and I embarked on public talks and media interviews.

Meanwhile, my life and spiritual path was moving increasingly towards healing. My own experience both as a therapist and woman led me naturally towards a more spiritual approach to wellness and psychological health. I continued to find personal solace in my soul home in Connemara, to which I returned frequently for increasingly longer periods at a time. I knew intimately the healing properties of a life lived close to nature and relished my time there. In between my clinical practice and rearing my children who had adapted well to life in Ireland, I took time to write. I would undertake short periods of solitude so as to fully immerse myself both in my inner world and to the voice of my soul. A failed relationship catapulted me into a search to heal my heart and to understand the journey to spiritual wholeness. I seemed destined to write about heartbreak. Four years later, *Love in a Time of Broken Heart* was written and published. Considering love as both a human and divine passion, in it I explored how our love relationships reflect our inner drive to wholeness, and how a love wound is a sacred initiation with opportunities for soul growth. Explaining the connection between our early life experiences and our patterns in love relationships and addressing the emotional turmoil resulting from relationship breakdown, this was perhaps my most personal book. By truly embodying the experience of heartbreak and the longing for love, *Love in a Time of Broken Heart: Healing from Within* charts the inner journey to healing and wholeness after heartbreak.

In the years that followed I was to throw myself into the world of soul healing, and created a personal if unique way of blending depth psychology with spirituality in my therapeutic practice. As the subtitle to *Love in a Time* suggests, Healing From Within became the primary focus of my workshops going forwards. My workshops and seminars became less focused on the theories of depth psychology than on spiritual wisdoms from sacred poets and writers. I had understood at a deeply visceral level, that healing oneself is less a matter of cognitive understanding than on feeling – on surrender, acceptance and love. As a Jungian I was no stranger to the power of the transcendent or the numinous to alter our consciousness and transform our lives. I understood very well the formative impact of our early years on our later patterns of behaviour and belief systems. The child maketh the man was true, but not definitive. We had the power to heal ourselves and change our consciousness, this all the more when realising our wounds are merely conduits to our growth. I had begun to see my own painful childhood and life experiences less as limiting but more as spiritual tasks of empowerment. And I knew in my deepest being that every heartbreak is a call to consciousness and to entering into a deeper experience of and appreciation of oneself.

It was during a difficult period in my own life that I encountered a woman, a Spiritual Teacher who was to change my life forever. A little before I settled full time into my 'soul' home by the sea, I had met and worked with Sai Maa, Spiritual Master and healer with a mission of global enlightenment through practical spirituality and personal transformation. Sai Maa was born in Mauritius, she spoke French, my maternal language and I felt instantly drawn to her. A beautiful woman in both soul and body, she embodied for me the Divine Loving Mother. In her living presence one is surrounded by and filled with the most Divine, unconditional, rose-scented love. At the same time, since Maa is also a trained therapist as well as an energetic healer, she urged us, through her unique Journey of Profound Healing program, to awaken and grow spiritually through uprooting and healing unconscious early life patterns and negative belief structures. Her programs were truly transformational. I related well to her way of working since I was also a therapist and understood how the imprints of our early life live on in later life. As a Spiritual Master and Teacher Sai Maa was uncompromising, even ruthless in her pursuit to lead us into self-mastery and awakening to our spiritual mission and destiny. Her programs were intense, challenging and utterly transformational. You were asked to leave your persona as well as your phone, books and even your spiritual practice behind as you entered the temple of profound healing she created. There were to be no distractions to your inner journey to self-awareness and healing. You were laid bare – you came face to face with yourself, utterly vulnerable and open. Your ego dismantled, there was nowhere to hide. Sai Maa surrounds you with Divine love in such a way that allows you to be that vulnerable.

I grew greatly in the active years of working with her. Conversely, however, my personal life was catapulted into upheaval, upset and ultimately lasting, life-giving change. It took me a while to see that though. First, I was to face heartbreak yet again. The relationship I was in crumbled under the stress of tumultuous growth and change. Ultimately, I was growing, he wasn't – at least not in the same way. I knew that relationships often suffered or fractured completely when one of the partners worked with Sai Maa and were on a path of personal transformation. Likewise, partnerships of profound union would be formed through both souls working together to grow spiritually. Alas, that was not my case. Although I loved this man completely, I could not force him where he did not want to go. After a couple of years of unhappiness, of trying to make it work, we broke up so that when I made the move to live full time by the sea in my 'soul' home, I was alone. A period of two years followed when my reclusive nature took over and I happily succumbed to solitude, to a sometimes raw loneliness and the call of a wild heart. I say wild heart because all the while I was hurting from a love wound, but deep down I knew my heartbreak would take me to a deeper knowing, a deeper loving. It was easy to follow the inner calling I spoke of earlier. I plunged myself into 'work', into reading copiously on spirituality, healing, depth psychology and of course my greatest love, poetry. I read and reread the love poems of Rilke, Rumi and the writings of the greatest mystics. John of the Cross's *Dark Night of the Soul*, which was never far from my bedroom, took up permanent residence on my bedside table along with Teresa of Ávila, Rumi, Kabir, TS Eliot, Emily Dickinson and others. By day I walked in nature and by the sea with my faithful companion, my dog. She seemed to relish our seclusion, curling up before a roaring fire when the wind howled and rain pelted the land. I continued to see clients and teach online, all the while sharpening my inner knowing, and increasingly moving towards and finding both answers and solace in the spiritual realm.

I travelled and spent time in India and the Far East, relishing both learning from new cultures and the cocooning of yoga and spiritual retreats. Inspired by a lifelong desire, I visited Sai Maa's birthplace, Mauritius, and was enchanted. My meditation practice changed and became more focused on connecting with the Sacred Feminine, the Great Mother. I started to trust more, I grew softer in myself. I understood intuitively that I needed to work on self-forgiveness and I learnt to nurture myself in a new way. I did not see many people, being content with my own space, visiting my children, some of whom had moved abroad, a few times a year. My little grandchildren began to appear and this opened up a whole new life for me.

Being blessed with grandchildren and embracing myself as a grandmother has been one of the greatest benedictions of my life. I found that connecting with these little souls of my bloodline awakened in me the desire to teach and share with them the wisdom I had gained from a life fully lived together with an openness to learning from them. My earlier work in the field of pre- and perinatal psychology and the study of the formative impact of early life taught me that children are wise and closer to God than we are. I continued to travel and present my work at international conferences. I spoke at events and continued to write. Although still involved with pre- and perinatal psychology my work was evolving constantly and I found that more and more people came to see me with relationship problems, with spiritual heartache or soul loss. Healing heartbreak and understanding the inner dynamics of love relationships was part of my focus, as was helping clients move towards a sense of wholeness within – individuation in Jungian terms. It had become more and more clear to me that people were looking for spiritual direction in a world that had become devoid of soul. And that developing a spiritual outlook was essential to healing and emotional well-being.

My book *Love in a Time of Broken Heart: Healing From Within* had been published in 2008. By the end of the book I had begun to write about healing and wrote a draft I entitled *Healing From Within* which I presented to my then literary agent with a view to completing a new book. In it I would write about our need to heal our emotional wounds and give a framework for understanding how imprints from our early lives may influence our later lives. Using a unique blend of psychology and spirituality, *Healing From Within* was designed to guide readers on a journey to inner healing. Examining how soul patterns transmitted to us in early life influenced our relationships and later life, this book offered a framework for understanding how this truth plays out in our lives. I suggested that identifying our patterns in relationships would help us recover a sense of inner wholeness and spiritual purpose, by uniting our inner masculine and feminine energies. Incorporating insights drawn from the weaving of psychological and spiritual truths and using the power of myth to amplify our human journey to healing, *Healing From Within* offered, I believed, a fresh and unique perspective on inner healing, soul work, love, relationships and the in-depth and lasting healing of emotional wounds.

That book never got written because somehow life intervened and my draft was left aside. Until now. I see that although still perfectly valid, this present book has a different focus or rather I have taken a different route to the same destination. And I have gone much further. I have changed; my writing has changed. And perhaps the intervening years, eleven in all, were a necessity to bring me to a new consciousness which would inform my writing and teaching. My soul at that time had decided I had more 'living' to do. I had to experience more of life, of love, of heartbreak and struggle so as to inform my work. My own spiritual growth and evolution have changed my outlook. I rely less on psychology these days than on spirituality, and more particularly on the natural spirituality of the earth, sea and animals. Whereas before the wisdom of the heart were words I understood, now, I fully lived them. I knew that to be wholly embodied meant living from the heart and acknowledging both our human and divine natures. I believe that change and personal transformation can only happen if we surrender, if we forgive, if we love. I know that despite the best will in the world, simply uncovering our wounds does not guarantee healing, because healing is a matter of the heart involving love, acceptance and surrender. Almost thirty years as a therapist and my own life experience have taught me this salient fact. One can spend years in 'therapy' or counselling, have a cognitive understanding of the experiences that have traumatised and caused us to shut down, and still not heal or move on. We can tell and retell our story, and have it witnessed and acknowledged by our healer/therapist, time and again, and still nothing happens. And nothing will, that is, until you allow the miracle to take place in your heart – the miracle of love and forgiveness. The natural world, the wisdom and unconditional love that animals can teach us, the new sciences all agree that the answers to health and emotional well-being lie in our own hands. The unconditional love that the mystics wrote about, the essential spiritual truths lived by the Gnostics and others who felt and lived God rather than paid lip service to an intellectual understanding of God, all point to the same thing. The answers to our life problems lie within. We were born with God in our DNA, we all have a Divine nature, whether we are awakened to this fact or not. Most of us have become separated from our divine self, and this is the cause and root of our suffering. And so, the key to healing is to go within and awaken our inner healer, experience the God within, join forces with our higher selves and realise that we are beings of light.

In a time of spiritual awakening, emotional healing must move beyond psychology if it is to be effective. I have no doubt of that. *The Soul & The Sea* presents a new model of healing based on an interweaving of depth psychology with spirituality. In doing so, the book reflects a universal call to awaken to the Sacred Feminine, to the Goddess within that had been banished from our hearts and whose time has now come. Understanding that healing is fundamentally a spiritual process requiring nothing more than our openness and willingness to love is perhaps the essential message of this book. Unconditional love and compassion, together with the courage to live our lives with spiritual elegance will carry us through the darkest night on the way to spiritual awakening and emotional healing. Connecting with the eternal healing wisdom present in all of life and most especially in nature is critical. You will find nature laced through the pages of *The Soul & The Sea* and be awed by her healing power. That is my hope. Additionally, as guide on the healing path, I offer my own journey and the stories of souls that struggle as we all do. In writing this book I have been informed not simply by my training and experience in depth psychology but also by my life experiences and studies in various fields. My knowledge of shamanic cultures, training in Curanderismo medicine and herbalism all form an integral part of my soul journey and are crafted into this book. Further and deeper heart learning has come to me through my lifelong love of poets and writers, especially Rumi, but also Rilke, and various Jungian authors. Most especially, however, it is my 'knowing', my own personal and intuitive experience of the Divine that has guided me in writing this book. I am grateful for the awakening in me over time of my inner Goddess and the sacred knowing of my many past lives as spiritual healer, sacred initiate and teacher. Since intuitive knowledge cannot be explained in a rational way, it took me some time to trust this knowing. During these last years, and most especially in the short period of writing this book, intuitive sacred knowledge was available for me to download so that in giving form to my book, I have allowed my dreams, meditations and intuitive knowing along with the poet and creative writer in me as much rein as my knowledge and clinical experience as a depth psychologist. Combined with a natural weaving of my own personal healing journey, this book aims to share my teachings as well as to inspire fellow soul pilgrims on their healing journey. *The Soul & The Sea* may offer those who read it insight and guidance into a journey of profound healing and spiritual growth. A deeply personal book, *The Soul & The Sea* bears testimony to the power of nature and our spirit to heal us.

Finally, I offer eternal gratitude for my deep-rooted connection with the sea and the land around my soul home in Connemara, Ireland.

Part One

Spirit of the Sea

Spirit of The Sea

Born by the sea, Magdalena's first cry broke through the waves
Of her mother's pain
And danced on the tide
That came and went on the beach below
Sucking the earth to a watery home
And lashing at the walls of her father's house
Perilously built on the edge of the world

As the winds carried the news to the outside and ends of the land
Touching down on the rugged edges
To the still even plains of green
Storm birds, alerted by their elders and the last sea eagles
Of Skye answered the call and gathered at their long abandoned
    nesting place
A hallowed ground housing a shaggy assembly
The Great and the Good, the old and the young
They came in their groups, landing on the cliff site
Folding their wings against their bodies
They stood in reverence
Awaiting the call

And it seemed that the earth itself had given birth
With a triumphant cry that stirred the slumbering roots
And quickened the guardian souls
Of ancient wisdom
Spirits of the forests and Sacred places awakened as though from
    a deep sleep
And stood to attention
Listening
Listening to the pulse of the earth and the Spirit of the Sea
As it spoke

It was said
A new soul had been born with the deep 'knowing' of the Ancients
in her bones
And the gift of sight
A knowing long gone from the earth and buried
Under the deep Atlantic
Out of sight of man or beast
Awaiting the return of Spirit to the earth
Magic and the gift of enchantment would return to the land
It was said

The gift of Insight would both bless and curse this child
For the Spirit of the Sea comes at a price
And not many can carry its weight
Or speak its language
Since the heart of man is frail
And clay feet cannot fly
Or touch the stars

Born on Divine wings
Spirit must soar through earth and matter
And not die or be afraid
And she who carries this power must use it well
Or be destroyed by it
She should climb the highest mountain
And dive into the deepest ocean
Drinking from the fountain of knowledge
She must gaze into the timeless well
Of life
And recount God's teachings
To all mortals who will listen

Spirit of the Sea takes no prisoners
And Magdalena grew to know this

And feel it in her body
So that each time she fell
She picked herself up
And continued reaching for the stars
Whose light bent low
For this child of God

And though sharing this humble trail
With many others
Magdalena understood she must travel
A fearless and intrepid path
And where there was no path
She must forge her own
And grow used to the sense of aloneness
All warriors face

And like all souls who walk this earth
Magdalena would have to forget
And be awakened
So that dark nights would have to be endured
And suffered
Until sight and stars returned
To light her way

****

Many earth years have passed
And weathered the land
Spirits and sea birds have come and gone
Carried on the mists of time
Now on the beach below Magdalena's house
The tide comes and goes sucking the earth to a watery home
Lashing at the legs of the land
Sea eagles and storm birds alight on the overhanging cliffs
And rest awhile,

Spirit of the sea still dances
And on quiet nights can be heard calling all those with the gift of
Sight

Remember me,
Remember me

Magdalena born by the sea
Whose first cry broke through her mother's pain
And was carried on the tide that came and went
Knows
She knows that Spirit of the Sea will dance yet
Long after she herself has passed to another realm
And that she will visit these western shores
Dancing on the tide that comes and goes

– Benig Mauger

Chapter One

Secret Places

Lovers find secret places
inside this violent world
Where they make transactions with beauty

Reason says, Nonsense.
I have walked and measured the walls here.
There are no places like that.
Love says, there are.

Reason sets up a market
And begins doing business
Love has more hidden work.
– Rumi

It seems to me that a large part of my creative soul has lived in a secret place for a long time. And that the essence of my work as a therapist, spiritual teacher and writer comes from a more hidden intuitive space than was apparent when I originally conceived this book. Try as I might follow a linear, more academic or structured plan, when I set about writing the book, I felt blocked. Words didn't flow well; the energy wasn't there. I struggled against this block for some while until one day I just gave up and went with 'the flow' which was pushing its way into my consciousness, mainly through my dreams, walks by the sea and periods of meditation and reflection. The result of this inner to outer stream is crafted into the following chapters. As a creative writer I am of course no stranger to intuitively inspired work but incorporating this dimension into a book on depth psychology and healing was new to me. Or so I thought.

Many years ago, when I was training as a psychoanalytic psychotherapist, I had an interesting experience perhaps presaging my propensity to engage in 'hidden work'. As trainees we were obliged to attend supervision where we presented client cases for discussion and analysis by our personal and group supervisors. During our training years, supervisors, tutors and personal analyst gauged our progress and development as therapists so that their input was required when assessing our readiness to qualify and begin clinical practice. When one of my supervisors was asked to comment on me, he said, "She does very good work, but she doesn't know how she does it!" This language, along with my therapist's report which stated that I had a "therapeutic personality", which whilst not quite considered heretical, nonetheless did not fit into the narrow framework of the Institute norms. That notwithstanding, I went on to qualify with the rest of my year.

Over time, I guess I have grown into myself as a weaver of secret or hidden work. I have always had a keen intuition, being born into a family with a long line of psychic intuitives on my mother's side. One of my aunts I believe was a water diviner whilst others were healers. I myself seem to have inherited this gift although not fully recognised at first. There is a story my mother used to recount. I had been given my first (analogue) watch at the age of eight which, after I would wear it for a short while, would go berserk and race forwards. My mother took it to a local watchmaker who told her the watch had been magnetised and enquired whether its owner was a nurse or radiographer. There were other occasions too many to mention, when my sensitivity and 'psychic intuitive' powers kicked in. But like most youngsters, I soon learnt to squash, hide or otherwise distrust my intuitive or psychic skills, only discovering and cultivating them later in life. It seems that unbeknownst to me, my work as a therapist was perhaps the beginning of my journey as an intuitive healer.

Therapy, Healing and Love

Therapeutic work is largely intangible. It is more often the personal qualities and empathetic nature of the therapist than their theoretical knowledge that enable clients to heal and grow. Just as in the words of the poet Rumi above when he writes, "love has more hidden work", therapy too is largely an invisible, hidden process. And so is healing. We don't always know how we do it, but it happens, and we 'do' heal. In fact, 'do' is the wrong word. I feel that healing is largely a matter of surrender, of love, and of such spiritual qualities as acceptance, forbearance and forgiveness. Of course, becoming psychologically conscious involves our intellects, our awareness and our willingness to delve deeply into the terrain of our souls. Psychoanalytic training helps us with this task in providing a theoretical framework within which to work. Although I could not have voiced it then, there is no doubt that as a trainee and young therapist, my intuition guided me just as much as my clinical training in my work with clients. But intuition, which can be described as an inner knowing that cannot be explained by rational means, did not hold pride of place in a 'scientific' training, hence doing good work but not knowing how I did it! Luckily for me, my supervisor understood and appreciated that particular quality in my work even if he also suggested I sharpen my more rational, theoretical skills.

Love in many ways is equally intangible; there is no rational explanation for love except that we are born as love and therefore its memory lies somewhere in our psyches. Despite this, however, many of us have forgotten or have not (yet) awakened to our Divine natures, to the part of us that is love. The words of the poet George Herbert echo – *"Love bade me welcome, yet my soul drew back, guilty of dust and sin."* There is a gap, a break somehow between our spiritual natures and our sense of being inherently wounded and maybe unworthy. When I was writing my last book, *Love in a Time*, it became clear that what was keeping us wounded, what was holding us in a place of fear, was our sense of separation. Our feeling of isolation from a bountiful force, from God, from our higher selves is in essence the source of our suffering. When we perceive ourselves and the world from the perspective of the ego, we are separate entities. When, however, we perceive the world from a spiritual or soul perspective, we are all one and part of the same Source or Divine matrix. It is easy to see that our interconnectedness and expanded consciousness makes healing, forgiveness and love accessible, whereas when we are fragmented, see ourselves as separate and are identified with our ego, our consciousness is limited thus making healing more difficult. Digging deeper, I think an intrinsic sense of unworthiness common to all humans appears as a shield against loving and forgiving ourselves. Whilst the complaint of many souls in therapy is not being able to 'find' love or feel truly loved unconditionally, as one expects to be as a child, rarely is the question asked of ourselves, "How well can I love?"

It took me a long while in my own therapy to realise how I might be blocking love, and hence, my own healing. My therapist would often tell me that I was 'hard on myself' or that I was like 'an empty ocean', all of which fell on deaf ears at the time because I was not yet ready to hear that. "Love has more hidden work": Love and indeed forgiveness lie in those secret places perhaps drawing from us more than we are able or prepared to give at any given time. Soul trekking asks us to go deep, to be fearless in our search and to accept without judgment what comes. And we will undoubtedly always encounter roadblocks by way of the ego on our journey, no matter how open we may be. We might not even recognise what is blocking us until one day, when we have ventured deep enough into the forest, love comes to us, just as simply and suddenly as a sun ray shining through the trees. In the words of the poet Rilke:

And how might Love have come to you? Did Love come like sunshine, like the glow of blossoms? Did it come like Praying? Tell!

In the following chapters you will read a good rational explanation for our psychic wounding by way of examination of our early life. There is no doubt that uncovering the origin of our wounding helps us become more conscious and therefore more whole. Depth psychology is all about making the unconscious conscious in the service of what CG Jung termed 'individuation' or coming into wholeness. Trekking our soul and bringing forth our complexes will indeed help us become aware of why or when we may have 'shut down' or developed behaviour patterns or belief systems that no longer serve us. But does this knowledge heal us? I am not sure. In my many years as a therapist I have moved from psychoanalyst to shaman, and from depth psychologist to spiritual teacher. I consider myself midwife to the soul. At some level I have understood that healing oneself is not a matter of will but of the heart. We cannot tell ourselves for example, "Now I will heal," but if we surrender to the process and allow our hearts to open and to suffer consciously, engaging with the process, we are well on the way to healing. In my own experience, one can remain at the cognitive level and never heal. Telling and retelling our story and having it witnessed by our therapist not once but many times may not result in feeling healed. Why? Because healing, like love, lies in those secret hidden places in our soul. Healing can come through in a dream, in a poem or when something outside us makes an electric connection, a resonance with something deep inside us.

My Soul and the Sea

For me, the sea holds the key to much of my healing. Walking by the sea melts some hardness, some knot in me and opens my heart. It is as though she, the Divine Feminine, the Mother, opens her arms and envelops me so that I become one with her. As a child I used to imagine I was a mermaid, and on our trips back from the island hoped to see one of my sisters perched on a rock combining her hair. She could explain to me what I was doing here and perhaps answer some of my girlish questions. Other times I would simply lie down on the ground and ask my (earth) mother to hold me. I would lie there until something magical happened, a doorway would open and I could feel my own heart beating with the heartbeat of the world. Not having a strong earthly connection with my physical mother due in large part to my birth in very difficult circumstances, it isn't hard to understand that the earth, the sea and the elements became my mother. I am not unique in feeling this way; I have encountered many other souls who felt as I did.

In the next chapters I also write about our chakra system and how our birth, womb and early life lay down patterns that can be seen embedded in our chakras. Chakras are energy portals within the body that provide the vital life force necessary for physical, emotional, and spiritual functions. The root chakra is the primary stabilizing force for the energy body that brings in nourishing vital energy to fuel most of the body's energetic needs. It helps us feel supported, secure, and able to move forward in our life. Our root chakra is the source of our physical connection to the planet, and in biological terms governs our adrenal and immune systems. If our birth and early life has been insecure or we have had a dodgy start in life, we may suffer fears and anxieties relating to our physical safety, we may feel ungrounded and suffer imbalances in the root chakra.

That was my case. Born at thirty-two weeks gestation, very small and premature, I was not yet ready for the world. I spent two months in an incubator with my chances of survival described to my mother as fifty/fifty. Spending a long time in the neonatal care unit of the local hospital meant I did not readily feel part of my birth family when I did eventually come home. Years of therapy and many tears later, I came to understand the impact my birth and early life had on me and my development as the person I am today. Although I have grown hugely in every way over the years, that tiny baby is an intrinsic part of me. So too is my natural affinity with nature and my spirituality. I feel my traumatic birth and insecure early life constellated in me a strong spiritual connection which informs me daily. In my work as a therapist and teacher I always hold that our wounds are conduits to our healing all the while knowing the painful conditions of my earliest life have led me to choose a therapeutic path. I am grateful for the learning that came from my birth experience which has taken me on the trail to helping others just as it revealed to me my destiny as a therapist and spiritual teacher.

Trusting the Intangible

Secret or hidden work is hard to quantify, and even harder to explain or pin down. Despite knowing what we know, we have a need, a desire for the concrete which is hard to shift. We feel if we don't 'see' something or if there is no tangibility for us to cling to, nothing is happening. And yet, one day, after perhaps years in therapy sitting on the same chair week in, week out, a miracle happens, a doorway opens and a great surge of love sweeps over us and we know we will never be the same again. Our malaise, our sense of being stuck, our pain has evaporated, and where we were blind we can now see clearly. Visibly, something (intangible) has shifted. The secret place has been discovered and the work that was hidden is revealed, enabling us to move on. Such I think is the secret of healing. There is a process, a timing involved that only the soul or the heart itself knows. As I said earlier, I can relate personally to this process in many ways but will share one with you here. During the many years of my analysis, my therapist and I would refer back to my earliest days in an incubator which we had identified as being a formative, if painful time in my life, responsible for many of my insecurities and sensitivities, and a particular sense of being 'separate' from others. During group therapeutic work especially in my training, I would sometimes feel that a glass/Perspex wall separated me from the others in the group and the world. Of course I had acknowledged this and knew that my therapist's gentle intervention suggesting I now "let go of the incubator" was sound advice. I thought I had. But one day, quite out of the blue, as I was climbing one of the rugged hills near my home, I stopped to rest briefly and leaned against a large granite rock. As I rested there, letting my breath return to normal, the words, "You don't have to carry the incubator around with you, you can let it go now," entered my head as though they had been spoken aloud. And I suddenly 'got it', the words were no longer merely words, something shifted and stirred and then settled in my heart so that I said out loud, "Right, so that's it, of course!"

Such is love, such is the healing process; and grace comes unannounced, without our bidding, sensing an openness within us. The Divine opens doors and offers us openings all the time; we don't often go through the doors, preferring instead the comforts of ego security. And since the ego feeds on separation, fearless courage and steadfast faith are spiritual qualities most of us have to develop. Patience and the ability to suffer and engage consciously with our souls, with our pain, with our confusion, is not a given. And yet this is what is demanded of us if we wish to heal our emotional and psychological wounds and progress on our spiritual path.

Body & Soul

When I first moved back to Ireland in the mid-1990s, I was asked to teach on several psychotherapy trainings. The head of department on one of these trainings asked me to devise a course that would include both the spiritual and psychological dimensions of healing and wellness. I did so, and called it Body & Soul. In this course, as well as laying out the theoretical basis for healing early life and traumas that created imprints, belief systems and psychological patterns in the individual, I was to include the etheric body, the energetic dimensions of healing and the chakra system. Since my psychoanalytic training encompassed Attachment and Object Relations theory as well as Jungian and pre- and perinatal psychology, I was not daunted by the prospect. Teaching depth psychology and traditional psychoanalytic theory was not difficult for me; what was more of a challenge was incorporating and blending together the spiritual and energetic healing modalities. There is of course an overlap between depth psychology and spirituality. In a sense, both can be said to be intangible, hidden work. Both require courage, openness and an availability to 'experience' life in all its vicissitudes and oneself as the flawed but beautiful human that we are. I believe that our onwards journey to healing involves not merely insights from depth psychology and an ability to examine our inner lives, but also prayer, meditation and other spiritual mediums. Spending time connecting with and communing with our inner world is as vital as taking physical medication to heal the body. Science has now moved on to accepting that our thoughts and our feelings can affect or even create our physical health and reality. And further, that we can, in actual fact, heal ourselves. Expanded and elevated consciousness can define our lives and create lasting changes on all levels. Such knowledge is now taking hold as we move through a time of transition to a new age of consciousness, the Aquarian age.

Written entirely during a world pandemic, this book bears witness, I believe, to the immense resilience of the human soul in the face of adversity. And the power of our minds to create change and heal not simply ourselves but our planet. More and

29

more souls are awakening to our true natures as divine beings of light and to our collective humanitarian mission.

Explorations into the nature and capabilities of human consciousness are not new. Scientists, authors and researchers in the fields of biochemistry, biology, and quantum physics all point to a form of central intelligence present in all of nature as well as an interconnectedness between all of life including humans. Author Rupert Sheldrake writes about Morphic Resonance and says that it is "the idea of mysterious telepathy-type interconnections between organisms and of collective memories within species" and accounts for phantom limbs, how dogs know when their owners are coming home, and how people know when someone is staring at them from behind. Advances in the field of psychoneuroimmunology show that the cells of the body can feel 'sad' and that when we feel depressed or sad our immune system suffers. They have shown that when people feel loved or are in touch with love they tend to be healthier physically and that single people suffer more flus and colds than couples in happy relationships! I have personally experienced this. One particular summer when I was suffering from the ending of a relationship and feeling very sad and hurt, I developed a chest infection which simply would not clear up, despite having recourse to much despised antibiotics! In autumn of that year my mother passed away, exacerbating the great sadness and grief in my heart. I went from cold to cold and chest infection to chest infection for some six months.

In conclusion, the thinking that we are all one and interconnected is, I feel, at the core of healing and being able to heal. We are part of a unified source, there is part of us made of starlight, and so psychology and spirituality are interconnected. We need to blend the two disciplines so that we can restore what has become lost within us and so that we can become more whole. Daily prayer, affirmations and meditation together with journaling, dreamwork and self-analysis using the tenets of depth analytical psychology can help us on this journey to healing.

And so I begin. Having laid out the foundations of my book and what I want to teach and share, I put down my pen. That night I have a dream that I am entering a hidden Red Room. A hitherto unexplored room in my soul, I am being guided there by the Divine Mother, the Goddess.

Chapter Two

The Red Room

Last night I dreamt I was in a hidden Red Room: a beautiful ornate chamber containing all sorts of artefacts, relics of wisdoms and ancient feminine mysteries. I knew I belonged there; I knew it was my own Red Room, buried in a deep layer of my psyche that up to now I had not visited. Too preoccupied with outer affairs, I had not taken the time to find and step in to this beautiful room of my soul. And now, with a global health crisis in which we had been ordered to stay at home and withdraw from the world, I had the perfect opportunity. I breathed deeply, approaching my Red Room. The energies were so strong I approached with caution; I was aware of a sweet smell of roses, of amber, of jasmine and of holy oils. I sensed I was entering a sacred place, a place I instinctively knew.

The doorway was open. An old heavy wooden carved door, it appeared to be resting against the ornate vibrant red tapestry of the room's interior. There was a sense of the Orient, India or Egypt maybe. As I enter, a woman, dressed in rich colourful, long flowing robes is sitting at a table. She has a pen in her hand and I see she is writing on what appears to be parchment, at an old beautifully carved desk. On the desk are many papers and thick books piled to one side. Behind her I see stained glass windows of exquisite colour and design. The woman looks up as I enter and seems to be expecting me. "Welcome," she says, nodding to a chair which stands opposite her at the desk. I sit. She hands me a pen, equally beautiful yet simple, and says, "Write." We face each other, I see she is neither old nor young, with a timeless beauty and wisdom. There is a sense of serenity, of ancient wisdom and mystical splendour and I feel instantly at home. The desk appears to be of old olive wood and feels smooth to my fingers as I briefly run my hand over the surface.

Then she urges, *"Write about loneliness, about anguish and the dark night of the soul."*

I pick up the pen and write... soon I am walking by the sea and the Red Room melts away.

The Anguished Soul

It is... only in the state of complete abandonment and loneliness that we experience the helpful powers of our own soul.
– CG Jung

One day, during my period of seclusion and mourning some years ago, I was walking on the beach below my home. The sky above was heavy with dark, almost black clouds that seemed to lean heavily on the sand, and although there was as yet no rain, I sensed a storm would not be long in coming. I hurried along, eager to get home safely before what would surely be heavy, driving rain. There was a great beauty in the dark clouds as they rested against a calm, almost still grey sea. It was perhaps two hundred metres to my house and I walked hastily, keen to avoid the soaking that comes quickly and abruptly when the Atlantic skies open. There was almost no wind, despite the impending storm. In my melancholic state, I paused and looked up at the sky and was reminded of the darkness that fills and surrounds us during our dark nights of the soul. I took a picture with my phone that I was to use later for one of my webinars. Most of my work is inspired by nature and I instinctively felt this beautiful if threatening image of darkness and approaching storm would symbolically represent the dark night, or the dark sea journey we are all asked to navigate during our earthly lives. Times of inner confusion and darkness we would rather not have to encounter in a world preoccupied with the pursuit of material objects and happiness which we mistakenly project on to the outer world. Even though most of us are afraid of these dark nights as immortalised by poet and mystic John of the Cross and others, our souls, our hearts, are designed to bear them. A part of me knew this, but it didn't stop the fear and the dread from appearing. Mystics and spiritual masters have immortalised dark nights as times of immense soul growth; a time when we encounter a deeper wisdom and hear a new voice, that of our deepest soul. I also knew from my studies of Jung that it is during a period of intense loneliness and abandonment that our inner wisdom surfaces. Despite knowing these truths, until you experience them, you really cannot truly know or feel any confidence that you will overcome the crisis and emerge a better person.

> *"One day you finally knew what you had to do, and began,"*
> writes poet Mary Oliver from "The Journey",
> *"though the voices around you kept shouting their bad advice –*
> *though the whole house began to tremble and you felt the old tug*
> *at your ankles,"*
> she continues.

And so I begin.

I am no stranger to dark nights of the soul. I know well about seclusion and the endurance necessary during periods of dark introspection. Neither am I a stranger to a soul anguish I can only describe as a gnawing loneliness and feeling of abandonment in the face of uncertainty. The dark clouds in the sky that day appeared at first like a threat but on reflection their beauty merged with the calmness of the sea below, and mirrored, it seemed to me, the confused state of our hearts when confronted by what we may perceive as an act of 'terror' from within us that we have no control over. A dark night may appear suddenly after an outer event that shatters our life as we have known it; it may creep up on us when we have 'let our guard down'; it may take us unawares so that we may wonder where this darkness comes from. Whatever way it manifests itself, the dark night of the soul is usually unwelcomed, often resisted, and always deeply unsettling. And yet, in the deepest core of our being, if we allow it, there is often a part of us that knows this is right, that this turbulence is an opportunity to jump into the abyss and take our chances on creating a new reality. And whilst we may also simultaneously long for or feel nostalgic for the comfort of the old life, there is a small star part of us that wants to leap forwards through the doorway offered us by our dark night of the soul. There is a call we suddenly hear, the call of our deepest being. Our soul wants something different or something more from us: it may want us to live a larger life, to open our hearts more, to attend to an inner calling we had up to now refused to answer. And so, we are pulled within to listen to our inner voice and in turn to what the collective soul might be wanting from us. It may take time to see the transformational or numinous quality of the dark night or indeed accept that there is a 'silver lining' to our experience, but if we really pay attention, there is no doubting the numinous power of this time.

In my own life such a soul call has often come in the form of a love wound, sometimes the end of an intimate relationship, the passing on of a loved one or a brutal family rejection. In the resulting sense of abandonment and desolation, I am catapulted directly into a dark night through which I am forced to navigate. As a deeply feeling woman, I have struggled at times with the intensity of my emotions. I have had to work at not allowing myself to be totally overwhelmed by my feelings. And yet, paradoxically, I have learnt that it is precisely my deep feelings that have acted as beacons to my creative heart. I write from the star in my heart; that is what guides me and my creativity. It is as though by following the intensity of my feelings, I open and walk through the doorway of the divine. I access the spiritual through my deepest feelings, through nature and my proximity to the sea. I have become aware of this over time. There is a great beauty in our deep emotions, human responses that at soul level take us to profound divine connection and the wisdom therein. At that time, walking on the beach those years ago, my heart was filled with sorrow and loss, and simultaneously the longing to connect with a great love, a soulmate. And although I had grown used to the gnawing loneliness of being without my lost love and partner, the rawness of my longing still took me unawares. It felt like I was being attacked from within. What surprised me conversely, however, was how this gnawing sense of loneliness simultaneously produced a great longing for love and for a connection which I experienced as life-giving. And although it seems strange to think in terms of dark acts of terrorism as life-giving, that's how it felt. It was as though my search for love and connection was being answered in some as yet obscure or intangible way and I gained some comfort from that. Human anguish and the deep soul searching that is part of a dark night are in themselves aspects of a spiritual trial that will lead to endless new possibilities and a new life. A sense of depression or desolation appear on the surface to be 'negative' emotions, but if we reflect deeply, they are responsible for propelling us into a new, much needed soul reality.

During my period of deep soul searching and self-isolation, I had learnt that I was being expanded. Inwardly, I knew I was growing, and that if I just surrendered, there was a greater plan at work in my life – even though I could not yet see it. I had to trust that I was being taken care of; it was all that was left to me, along with my tears and search for love. I meditated and walked by the sea to keep my heart open. My connection with nature is such that I instantly come back to my centre, and to my heart when I am outside and especially by the sea; it feels like I resonate with the heartbeat of the world. The constancy of nature with its eternal cycles connects me with my own beating heart and ancient soul. The trees, waves, shoreline, cliffs and fields seem to open a doorway to the divine through which I walk gladly. The healing energy of nature cocoons me. In a state of openness and expanded awareness grace can enter and peace can descend. It was thus for me at this time. I thought of the wise words of Sufi masters and others who extol soul longing as a true path to God or to our higher consciousness. *"I come empty handed, bringing to you nothing but my desire to receive your gifts. Fill my soul."* During my daily readings I had learnt that the yearning to love is a catalyst to great spiritual searching. And this longing for union with another soul is universal and the living imprint, as the poet John O'Donohue writes, of God's desire for us and ours for God, or the Divine. *"Our longing is an echo of the Divine longing for us. Our longing is the living imprint of Divine desire."* I resonated deeply with this knowing. Sufi master and poet Rumi's words, *"What you are seeking is also seeking you,"* were and still are, an essential sacred truth I live with and gain comfort from during difficult times.

Going Deep: Enduring the Dark Night

No matter how 'evolved' and self-aware we may feel, a period of desolation or intense depression is often an intrinsic part of the journey to spiritual healing and growth. Dark nights of the soul provoke deep questions; our life as we know it may cease to make sense. We are surrounded by an unwelcomed metaphorical death and darkness which we find hard to endure and which we normally fight or at least resist. Everything we thought was secure is no longer so; instead of inhabiting a house of bricks we find we are living in a house of straw that can be blown away at any time. In my last book, addressing the dark night of the soul, I wrote:

We are no strangers to death. Psychologically we suffer (ego) death frequently in the process of becoming conscious. Death is a great leveller, the dark night is like death in that everything we know is dissolved, our castles are destroyed, and our dreams smashed. We can only let go, and surrender – awaiting the dawn of a new day – awaiting a new life.

Even though from a spiritual perspective, the dark night is a very beautiful and sacred process, it can be perceived at the time as both harrowing and difficult. Especially when you are in the thick of the fog. You may feel as if you are stuck in the dark with no hope of seeing the light again. You already feel totally alone, and on top of that, darkness is not often talked about in traditional spiritual texts. Many of us look for the light only, and try to run away from the dark, not realising that the dark will only grow larger the more you ignore it. That is where the depth psychology and more specifically Carl Jung's writings and teachings on the shadow are so helpful. Jung tells us to become aware of and consciously integrate the shadow in the service of individuation or coming into a sense of wholeness. In other words, he affirms the life-giving and transformational elements of the dark night of the soul. Another Jungian author I know speaks of finding the light in the darkness. Grappling with our shadow (which can also be described as our dark side) is part of the psychotherapeutic process to ultimately bring us into a place of wholeness within.

Alchemy

Jung used alchemy and more particularly the alchemical stages as a metaphor to describe the psychological process of navigating the dark night of the soul. Specifically, Jung related the dark night to the alchemical stage called the 'nigredo' or blackening. In this phase, the substance undergoing change is blackened by fire so it can be purified and broken down to its most basic constituents, also known as the 'prima materia'. Psychologically speaking, we can compare this to when a disruptive event in our outer life causes us to turn inward; to shed our outside, public-facing self, and confront our inner hitherto ignored self. This is when we enter the dark bewildering inner world of the unconscious, where we encounter what Jung called our shadow, or the previously unexplored 'dark side' of our personality. In his book *Alchemical Psychology: Old Recipes for Living in a New World*, psychologist and author Thomas Cavalli, PhD, writes:

> *Your garden, laboratory, church, or temple is not the place to find the prima materia used in personal alchemy. Rather, a good place to begin the search is in our mess, our crisis, our broken dreams, our worst nightmare, disasters – all those horrible experiences that are associated with the shadow aspects of life. That is where we are most vulnerable and most apt to summon up the courage to make dramatic changes.*[1]

During this stage, as we confront our disowned or suppressed shadow, we may also start to let go of attachment to our outward identity and worldly objects such as our body image, material objects, job titles, and even relationships. When we start to release the outer layers of our personality, we become more deeply acquainted with our true soulful selves. At this time, we can also become more attuned to our intuition and to the numinosity of our inner voice.

According to Jungian author Cavalli, the work of the nigredo stage is to integrate both the darkness and the light in our lives. An example might be someone who suffers a crisis of identity after losing a career or job. The period after the loss may force the person to confront not only feelings about being fired, but also herald in a time of deep soul questioning. Time spent in reflection may unearth suppressed shadow material – such as how the person may have become addicted to overwork to push away a sense of loneliness and low self-esteem. Or he may realise that he is a people pleaser, exhausting himself by trying to please everyone whilst leaving himself out. There may even be a realisation that he or she was doing the job or pursuing the career largely to obey a parental expectation rather than their own calling. Many people unconsciously live and work following a norm or pattern as dictated by societal and familial expectation. If the dark night results in an identity crisis all the better, since the sufferer will undoubtedly emerge with greater self-knowledge and possibly a newer, more authentic identity. When the darkness of the shadow comes to consciousness, it can be integrated with the light or the more conscious, life-affirming qualities of a person. This, in turn, can drive the person forward into making more informed choices that truly support his or her authenticity, wholeness, and well-being. In other words, a dark night may be exactly what an individual needs to become a more whole and integrated, congruent person, living an authentic life.

I knew this was true for me after my relationship ended. I had to let go of not just my past partner, but of the life I had thought we would live together. I had to let go of the plans I had had for our joint life. In retrospect I can see that my dark night of the soul had been given to me as a way to force me into seclusion so I could ultimately connect with my deepest self. I knew that being a passionate woman who often lost herself in her lover, I had a tendency to give all my energy to love relationships, at the expense of my own being. My feminine soul was calling me, I have no doubt of that. Thankfully, I answered the call even though every fibre of my tender heart wanted to be with my lost love (rather than with myself). After a while, as I have said previously, the peace, serenity and wisdom I found gradually replaced the gnawing loneliness and sorrow in my heart. Replaced may not be the right word since I still experienced the pain and suffering of the dark night, but these periods became less and less as a gradual softening and settling nestled into my being. Navigating this dark night, I followed the beacon of my heart and gained great solace not just from walking in nature and by the sea, but in my daily readings, sacred poetry mostly. I devoured John of the Cross, Teresa of Ávila and some of the Sufi and Zen poets. Lyric FM became a frequent companion as did most instrumental classical music. As I continued my healing journey I wrote. Writing, or being able to write with ease was a skill I had discovered many years previously when I had undergone Jungian analysis. My therapist suggested journal writing and of course the writing of my dreams, a practice I continue to this day. I wrote poetry, copious amounts of it, and later the books I have since published. Most of all, my dark nights gave me my profound experiences of spiritual awakening which meant I developed a regular spiritual practice that I followed with love and reverence. I saw with new eyes; my spirituality became a central part of my being and supported my rich inner life. Transcendent consciousness informed me along with a deepening of my own mystical powers and intuition. It was as though a new door had been opened through which I walked gladly.

A dark night of the soul has a mystical or spiritual aspect and a profound psychological element. Defined as a period of spiritual desolation in which all sense of consolation is removed, the process is intangible and often alarming since we are launched into uncertainty and darkness. The religious or mystical view is that the purpose of the dark night of the soul is to strip us of our futile attempts to find God on our own terms and awaken us to a much simpler desire for intimacy with God. Mystics such as St. John of the Cross and St. Teresa of Ávila envisioned the dark night as a time of spiritual purging and illumination, but they also understood that psychological dynamics are often at play in a dark night experience. Though they lacked modern categories and definitions, they were some of the most adept psychological minds of their day, as is evidenced in their writings and poetry. God in their writings is a metaphor for our higher consciousness and awareness. In psychological terms, dark nights of the soul are about the dissolution of the ego. The letting go of what we thought we knew, the death of everything we thought was a 'given' in our lives plunges us into uncertainty and chaos. Life ceases to have meaning, and we cannot see a way through. A true dark night is not surface; it is deep and challenging and will take you away from the joy of your everyday life. In psychological terms it can be called a depression; in spiritual terms it is a sacred trial that will bring you to a new level of consciousness. One lesson we can learn from the mystics is that dark nights are not problems, but opportunities. Grasping this reality moves us beyond needing to find ways to get out of our dark nights to asking: *"What might I learn from this?"*

Letting Go: Ego Death

The ego is tough; it wants to be in control at all times and it is the ego's job to keep us separate from our true higher selves. For many of us it can be hard to really define what is ego and what is our true self. Our ego is the driver of our personality – it is in charge generally of our everyday lives. The Self, on the other hand, signifies the coherent whole, unifying both the conscious and unconscious mind of a person. What distinguishes classical Jungian psychology from earlier theories is the idea that there are two centres of the personality. The ego is the centre of conscious identity, whereas the Self is the centre of the total personality – including consciousness, the unconscious, and the ego. Our dreams, for example, usually come unfiltered by the ego since they are the voice of our soul that surface whilst we sleep; our soul's way of reaching us so that we can become balanced. The overarching function of dreams is to bring 'another view' into a picture that is seen through the lens of the ego, so that we can become more psychologically whole. And to point to our blank spots. The helplessness we feel during the dark nights of the soul is a complete anathema to the ego who thrives on being in control. Surrender and acceptance of what is, is not part of the ego's modus vivendi. Living with uncertainty is something most human beings fear greatly. It is a fact, however, that on emerging from a dark night of the soul you will become more of who you really are. You will become more authentic and congruent. It may be your purpose in life is to become 'awakened' to your true self and really live your life with a deep sense of purpose.

For me, emerging from a dark night has meant a new layer to my heart and soul. I can say I have grown each time and have been able to add extra dimensions to my being; in short, I have emerged with a renewed sense of self. Not a great lover of the term 'going with the flow', I was well into my journey of psychological and spiritual growth before I realised why. I, akin to many others, liked to think I was in control of my life. I believe that dark nights have appeared at various times to help me flow with life, not necessarily the life I want to live, but the life I am meant to be living. Sometimes we have to get out of our own way and let our life 'live us'. I believe that at some level, many of us are afraid of flowing with life's tide, so we fill it with all sorts of distractions, ego pursuits, ambition, relationships and addictions. A dark night may then appear, paradoxically, as a way to return to living and being in the flow. A dark night of the soul pares life down to its essentials and helps you get a new start. It is vital to realise, however, that the growth and transformation will only happen from within. No one chooses a dark night; it is given to us. That being said, as in the alchemical process, I believe our job is to live the dark night and sift it for its gold.

World Pandemic: Navigating Personal & Collective Dark Nights

Your dark night is an invitation to become a person of heart and soul.
– Thomas Moore

Jungian author Tom Moore suggests that dark nights invite us to become a person of heart and soul. To become more real and authentic. I feel this is true. Darkness and turmoil stimulate the imagination in a certain way and allow you to see things you might ordinarily overlook. I suggest that you do not spend the time fighting or trying to get rid of your dark night; you may not learn its lessons or go through the important changes it can fashion for you. The aim is not to try and solve the dark night but rather be enriched by it. During this crisis, there is no choice but to surrender control, give in to unknowing and listen to whatever nuggets of wisdom might come along. If you are still, you will hear another voice – that of your own soul. I have found that during these dark times – and when I am particularly vulnerable – a deeper intelligence comes through. I see dark nights as a time of enforced retreat and perhaps unwilling but beneficial withdrawal.

At time of writing, the world pandemic has offered us a dark night. Where it will lead us and what we will make of it has not yet become clear. Scared, anxious and forced into isolation, we are in unprecedented and very uncertain times. As we listen to the news we hear of untold suffering, of fear, of panic and heartbreak in the face of the coronavirus pandemic. As we are being asked to 'keep a distance' from others, we have paradoxically never felt so connected. We need each other, we send messages of support, we set up online connections like never before. In the loneliness of the social distancing measures we have had to adopt, we have realised what is important. The truth of John Donne's words "No man is an island" resonate deeply within our hearts. We realise that love, compassion and our connection with each other, with nature and with our spiritual source are what matter most. That the pandemic has come to teach us and bring us to a new level of consciousness is very clear. COVID-19 has certainly taught us that in essence, we are not in control. And that the world and the planet need us to change our direction from gross materialism to humanitarianism. People are aware of and embracing higher consciousness. Now is the time to put into practice, to 'animate' the spiritual teachings we have learnt. About all being one, about inner empowerment, about conscious co-creation, about how we can together create a new reality. Opening our crown (corona) chakras to our divine natures and the power of our spirit is crucial if we are to move forward to a new age – a new consciousness, the age of Aquarius.

What is clear is that dark nights force us beyond the everyday human, ego life, to encounter and open up to new mysterious possibilities. The willingness to engage and consciously take part in the transformation being offered to us means we must endure. We must consciously suffer. Conscious suffering brings about the sacred and opens us to the divine. Poet and playwright Oscar Wilde wrote to a friend of his own dark night after being released from prison:

My desire to live is as intense as ever, and even though my heart is broken, hearts are made to be broken; that is why God sends sorrow into the world... to me, suffering seems a sacramental thing, that makes those whom it touches holy – any materialism in life coarsens the soul.[2]

Oscar Wilde suffered keenly and has left us through his legacy of soulful writings a map of what it is to be wholly human, to love and to suffer. I often read *De Profundis* and *The Ballad of Reading Gaol*. To me they are deeply moving and two of the finest pieces of writing ever written about the vagaries of living, loving and being human. No doubt Oscar Wilde's soulful writings sustained him during his own dark night and period of incarceration in a repressed era and hostile world.

During times when our soul is anguished, we may need a gentle hand to hold us and to simply lift us and put us back on our path. For me, connecting with the sea, an embodiment of the Divine Feminine puts me back in alignment – almost right away. I remember sacred truths I may have forgotten and gain the courage to trust my inner voice, to trust my soul and wherever it is taking me. During dark nights, I learn to have confidence in and follow the beacon of my heart. And to have faith that there is a greater plan at work in my life, no matter how obscure that path may seem at any one time. I urge you to gravitate towards that which may sustain you in your own dark night, whether it be literature, music, walks in nature or bonding with what or who you love. Most of all, a dark night offers you the opportunity to fall in love with your own soul.

A tiredness overwhelms me, and I sense I am being called away. I put down my pen and go to my meditation cushion. Perhaps I will have another dream. It is dark outside, and the sea is calm.

Chapter Three

The Pink Room

Only when we begin to understand how vast the Mother is
Will we begin to understand how powerful she is,
And how powerful we, her divine children, can be when surrendered
to Her, guided by her, infused with her immense, passionate, and
Transfiguring sacred force.
– Anne Baring & Andrew Harvey, *The Divine Feminine*

I do not remember a dream. It seemed I had a quiet night although when I awoke the sea was agitated – I could hear her through my window along with a gentle yet increasingly robust and persistent wind. I wondered, was there a storm approaching? Atlantic storms being a regular occurrence I was not immediately concerned, although I sensed a change was about to happen. I was right. But that change had little to do with the wind or the outside world, it was within me. During my morning meditation, I experienced a stronger than usual connection to Mother Divine and the Goddess, in which she spoke to me directly. I had been at that time suffering from recurring sore throats and a lot of acidity in my system. My throat felt raw, and I was unsure if at a physical level I was suffering from a digestive disorder or indeed simply a throat virus. Or maybe both at the same time. I knew that I have had a very sensitive system since my birth, so digestive disorders were not new to me. However, at some deep level, I felt this was not the whole story. That despite treating my symptoms from a conventional medical physical perspective, and receiving no major or lasting relief, there was more to the story. My throat remained raw and sore, and I experienced like a closing in feeling every now and again. Could I be developing a new allergic reaction to food or something in my environment? Acutely sensitive to the electromagnetic and atmospheric adjustments currently taking place as our earth shifts during this stage of transition, I had a sense I could be simply mirroring changes happening on the planet and experienced by many others. I also knew that at a subtle yet profound level, my body is my barometer, and its symptoms often a reminder of what I am being required to do at a soul level. I needed to go within and listen to my inner self to find out what these symptoms were telling me.

I experienced a lot of fear during such times. Fear that there was something seriously medically wrong with me, and yet deep in my heart I knew this wasn't so. I cannot explain this awareness except to say, I am so finely tuned in to my body and physical symptoms that I can go within when I manage to push through the fear. I believe there is a guidance within our bodies and our emotions that is always available to us, if we are able to listen. In a way, fear is like a learning to me. When I get fearful, which is not often and usually only when I experience what I perceive as 'something wrong' with my body through experiencing physical symptoms, I do what we all do, I contract. And when we contract, we close down. This happens in many ways, but the most profound and far reaching is closing down to the Divine in us. In essence when we are in contraction, the opposite to expansion, we are not in touch with love or with the divine or pure part of us. We can also forget our soul's purpose. We begin to doubt and forget our spiritual connection, and in doing so, fall prey to all sorts of fears and blocks. My soul, wise and old that it is, knows this and so produces symptoms to 'pull' me inwards into looking at what is going on.

That is what happened on this particular morning. I settled on my meditation cushion and opened myself to receiving whatever guidance came.

Hecate: Crone, Wise Woman & Goddess of Transformation

I closed my eyes and focused on my heart. My throat was burning and very soon I could feel a great fire in my heart. As I concentrated, the flames of the fire grew larger and larger, and through them I saw a woman tied to a stake, screaming and crying in distress. I spoke with her, and took her down, cradling her in my arms. She begged me to "speak" for her – for all of us thus persecuted – and cried because she felt I had "forgotten her". I knew instantly she was me in a past, probably Cathar life, and that in essence I was unconsciously blocking her or blocking myself from letting her energy speak through me. The burning sensation in my throat and oesophagus became stronger as the flames expanded and finally came out through my mouth. *"Write, speak for us, the forgotten ones."* The Goddess appeared then and put a pen in my hand. *"You are no longer a baby, you are strong and full of energy, let me in."* She spoke strongly and yet with compassion. I understood. The reference to the baby was to the part of me that was consciously connecting in to my earliest experiences of being very premature and tube-fed in an incubator. I would have had a nasal gastric tube inserted since I was not mature enough to feed in the normal way. My oesophagus was burning now at this moment remembering, and I felt utterly vulnerable and small. My third eye began to hurt; I breathed into it and asked what was blocking it. *"You are; you are blocking through your fear, let me in, it is safe to let me in."* I heard her clearly, and I knew instantly this fear went way beyond this life, further back to previous lives of being burnt and persecuted for speaking out. The fear of expressing myself was lodged in my throat and blocking me from getting on with the task of writing my book.

Many of us in the healing profession, particularly as midwives, healers, herbalists, wise women, therapists or sages, had past lives that were persecuted and terminated, usually in a violent way. If we were channels for the healing feminine energy direct from spirit and the earth goddess, we were castigated the most. Those that spoke out for the spiritual truths they knew, were punished greatly. Back then, many people lived their spirituality or rather had a personal, experienced knowledge of God and the Divine. We call this Gnosis, which means a direct experience of God. Of course this 'direct knowing' was threatening to the orthodox church fathers who preached a patriarchal religion and adherence to strict laws and rules devised by themselves and which kept them in power. Personal spirituality is on the increase in modern life as more and more people are awakening to their divine natures and actively pursuing a spiritual path. However, the old wounds are there, deep in our cellular memory so that many of us today, who are similarly called to be healers and bearers of this feminine healing energy, have deep wounds that go back a long time to these lives where we were persecuted and killed for speaking out and practising our truths. Often a deep terror and paralysing fear blocks our throats from speaking out and our hearts from being able to love. We may have difficulty receiving divine guidance without fear of loss, reprisal or worse. This fear may be lodged deeply inside us, in our cellular memory, and so there is an unconscious apprehension, shame and a terror somehow of being discovered.

This was the case with me. My throat, my body was displaying symptoms as the cellular memories of my past were surfacing and coming closer to consciousness.

Some months previous to the time I am speaking of now, when I was experiencing again a myriad of physical symptoms that brought up my deepest fears and anxieties, I had plunged myself into reading books on the Goddess and the lost wisdom of Sophia. One particular book, *You Are a Goddess* by Sophie Bashford, grabbed me most particularly in her description of the Goddess Hecate, otherwise known as the Queen of the Witches and Goddess of the Underworld and the Crone. Hecate's origins are ancient and date back to the Goddess cultures of thousands of years ago. Hecate is the archetypal Crone or wise female elder. She represents the third age in a woman's growth, post menopause. As the guardian of the underworld, it is she that is sent to help us heal from our deepest and most terrifying wounds, deep in the unconscious. Hecate is known to come at a liminal time in our lives, when we are at a crossroads, and perhaps at a point of new spiritual emergence and growth. As a Jungian I was already very familiar with the use of myths and fairy tales as archetypal depictions of the underlying psychic currents or energies that inform our lives. That the energy of Hecate had been stirred in me was no surprise. I was and still am at the Crone stage in my life as a woman, being in my sixties and a grandmother. As an Archetype, Hecate or the Crone is the guardian of the unconscious and the one who is called to reveal to us our deepest and most profound wounds and guide us to their healing.

I was wounded in the throat and I instinctively knew that part of the problem was a fear of speaking my truth or of expressing myself. I was at the time struggling to write this book and finding it very hard to get started properly. I would begin, then find so many other things to do in the day, such as walk the dog, practise yoga, meditate, cook meals, clean the house and attend to the garden, that six o'clock in the evening would arrive and it was time for dinner and relaxing in front of the TV or to watch a film. I anguished and wrestled with the title so that I could not begin writing. If I didn't know the title how was I going to write? I knew what I wanted to write about but could not begin. As the recurring sore throats came to a painful crescendo, one sunny weekday, I called a colleague who took me through a process I can only describe as revealing and ultimately transformative. I was not feeling safe, I was lost, and crucially seemed unable to open to the divine within me.

I had lost trust, I feared that if I spoke up, I would encounter not simply hostility, maybe derision, but more devastatingly, reprisal and punishment. All this at an unconscious level, of course. So when the Goddess spoke to me and said, "Let me in," I understood. I opened my heart to her, we met, and we became one. I understood that as an archetype, she is a deep wise part of me and that she had come to somehow set me free. I realised I had been blocking myself out of fear, out of an unconscious terror that was rooted deep in my unconscious from many past lives as a healer or wise woman persecuted and killed. I had lost faith also in the Divine Feminine, Mother Divine, Goddess or God, to keep me safe and protect me. And so that afternoon, with my throat burning and a great fire in my heart, I asked God to love me and take care of me. *"I am innocent, I am whole and I am held in the arms of the Divine"* became one of my most precious and loved affirmations.

And so I write.

I am walking by the sea again and stare out at the blue, turquoise waves bathed by the sun as they gently lap up to the shore. I am wistful, thinking about a dream I had the night before, a dream in which my lost love comes to me; a soulmate I had loved and lost who passed away some years ago but who still comes to visit in my dreams. When he comes I know he has a message and it is usually about love. In this last dream he is on the telephone and I know it means he is trying to communicate with me. He tells me he will be back soon, so I feel happy and a little excited. Next morning in my meditation I am taken by the Goddess to a pink crystal cave. It lies at the bottom of the sea in a far corner of a vast beautiful ocean space. It is hidden from view and slightly elevated on some rocks and surrounded by coral. Inside the cave is all pink quartz and sparkling gemstones with rounded edges. I touch the stones and feel instantly loved and healed. At the very back of the cave, deep within, sits the Goddess. She is tall, dressed in a flowing gown and veil, white and light blue. At her heart she wears a large pink quartz stone encased in a silver frame which sparkles as it captures the singular ray of the sun. There is a delicate smell of roses. I enter and walk towards her. She welcomes me, and again, motions to a room through which I see a large desk on which are placed several gemstones of all colours, but mainly white and pink quartz. *"Welcome," she says, picking up a pen and handing it to me. "I have been waiting for you. Write about human and divine love, about heartbreak and about healing."*

I pick up the pen, I sit at the desk basking in the beautiful, unconditionally loving scent of roses. Soon the cave disappears and I am walking by the sea again.

Human and Divine Love and Sacred Heartbreak

I was destined to grow spiritually through my love relationships. Way back as a small girl, I remember asking my 'nana' to read my palms. As a young child I was often in the care of a local village woman who was considered a little strange since she was an 'orphan' and only had one hand. She was very poor, lived alone and spent time as the sacristan and cleaning lady for the local church. My mother employed her for a while as a maid, but her main work had been to look after me, since as I have already said, I was born premature and did not come home to my family until I was two months old. Being very small and somewhat delicate, Mary took charge of me when my mother was busy with the rest of the family. An unusual soul, Mary would tell me stories about angels, fairies, and more terrifyingly, the 'banshee'. A banshee is a female spirit in Irish mythology who heralds the death of a family member, usually by wailing, shrieking, or keening. She generally has long grey hair and walks the shores 'keening', a particular kind of mourning cry. However, she can also be a sorrowful or mystical young feminine figure lamenting death and loss of loved ones. When they manifest themselves, these banshees can appear as beautiful, enchanting women that sing a sorrowful, haunting song which is filled with love for their families. Fairies, both good and bad, which Mary said would steal me if my mother did not bring in my baby clothes from the drying line outside before dark, were very much a part of my early life. I guess I felt connected to nature and natural spirituality very early on and never questioned where God was; he or she was in the earth, the cries of the sea, the wind, the seagulls and the land around me.

One day, my 'nana' decided to read my palm. I didn't drink tea, being too young, so she couldn't read the tea leaves as was the custom with some village soothsayers or 'fortune tellers'. Taking my small hand in hers she turned it over and examined the tiny lines etched there. I remember two things. One, "You will have a very long life," and two, "You will be married at least twice"! This last was said in some humour mixed perhaps with some trepidation as marriage is sacred in the traditional Catholic church and divorce is a no-no. The idea that as a woman one would have more than one sexual partner and certainly one that wasn't one's husband, or that one would have more than one of those, was taboo. Nonetheless, back then in a small corner of rural Ireland, with someone I would with hindsight consider a native wise woman, I was not concerned. She showed no judgment whatsoever on what she had read, and I knew she loved me. I was a pretty petite little child with blonde hair and large brown eyes. Mary had told me I had deep soulful eyes and that if I concentrated enough, I would feel God (or the Goddess) moving through me. Now many years later, informed not simply by my life, but by my studies in Jungian psychology, I realise I was born an Aphrodite woman. This meant I would be focused towards attracting men and perhaps experience many love affairs. It would also undoubtedly mean I would experience heartbreak, perhaps many times in my pursuit of love.

Aphrodite: Goddess of Love, Beauty & Desire

What is an Aphrodite woman? Jungian archetypal psychology uses mythology as a metaphor for the human condition and to describe psychological aspects of our individual soul. The stories and antics of the Greek and Roman gods and goddesses serve as symbols and can hold some essential truth about who we are; their struggles mirror our own. There is something essential about myths and stories that mean something to us. Stories are the universal currents of history and contain archetypal energies that we resonate with at a deep unconscious level. Who is Aphrodite? Jungian author Arlene Diane Landau writes that the Aphrodite woman always stands out, she lights up a room; when she enters, heads turn. And it is not just a physical thing, there is something 'special' about an Aphrodite woman, she exudes joy, pleasure and beauty and incites desire. As Jungian author James Hillman says,

> *Psyche serves in the temple of Aphrodite. Aphrodite is what makes something light up so you want it. She's the touch of beauty.*[3]

The Greeks and Romans worshipped Aphrodite as the goddess of pleasure and beauty and were careful to place offerings to her. Beautiful buildings, tasteful good food and aesthetic surrounding were revered and considered an important adjunct to life and a sense of well-being. I can relate to this personally as I pay attention to my surroundings, always making sure to have fresh flowers around my home and working space, and beautiful pictures, crystals and shells. Some of my friends laugh at how I would wince if someone put a milk carton or packet of butter on the table at a meal. I always decant these onto nice dishes even when I'm on my own. As a woman I would pay attention to nurturing my body and my looks. For fifty years I have had a daily ritual of deep cleansing and face creams, a habit taught to me by another Aphrodite woman, my mother, and on which I spend a good deal of my budget. I would never dream of going out for dinner or to a social evening or event without dressing up, or at the very least donning a colourful scarf or other accessory, and it grieves me greatly if the person with me, particularly if he is a partner and male, doesn't do so. Even at my age, I consider that by making the effort to dress up and look good, I am honouring myself, my partner, and Aphrodite or the beauty principle.

But of course, as with every archetype, there is a dark side to Aphrodite which I will speak about later. A word here about archetypes. As defined by Jung, archetypes are universal images or energy forces that inform our lives. All humans have a common psychic structure (the collective unconscious) that is inherited. Within the collective unconscious are the unconscious images of the instincts, and Jung named these archetypes. Archetypes can also be described as energy forces that exert a powerful influence on our lives. Jung described the ability of the psyche to record and remember experiences which went far beyond the confines of biography through his concepts of the collective unconscious and the existence of archetypes which informed our minds and governed our behaviour. Gods and Goddesses are merely personifications of the archetypes. So having a lot of Aphrodite energy means that her qualities as described above are strong in a particular person, and will drive their behaviour and can be seen through their personalities. We all know people who are 'typical warriors' or leaders or 'dreamy artists' or mystics like Persephone or craftsmen like the God Hephaestus. It is important to note, however, that we are influenced by a great many 'Gods' and 'Goddesses', and inherited psychic imagery. The more conscious or self-aware we become, the more balanced and integrated we become. If we identify with the archetype and do not redeem other aspects of our soul, we will be unbalanced, and in the case of Aphrodite, may end up living out her dark side, endlessly driven by a false notion of love and beauty.

To go back to my central theme and my 'nana's' prediction. It seemed my destiny was sealed as an Aphrodite woman from a very early age. Love relationships, being in love and experiencing heartbreak many times would be my path. Many years and loves later, I was to write about this. In my book *Love in a Time of Broken Heart* I write,

> I seemed to have been destined to experience and write about love and the conflict of the heart. At the tender age of seventeen I found myself loving two boyfriends at the same time and wondering how it was that I was able to do this. Mindful of their feelings and given an ultimatum, I eventually chose one, the one who would eventually become my husband. However, the process was very painful for me and I can still recall the pain that my young heart had to go through. I remember that I cried solidly for three days. Perhaps this was the beginning, in me, of really experiencing loss which making a choice always demands.[4]

In fact, Mary's palm reading all those years ago proved to be true and I did marry twice. By the time I was forty-three I had three children, been married and divorced twice, and was still being enchanted by love. I was attracting and enchanting men, and suffering through intense and passionate love affairs. I had married very young. Liberated from the constraints of marriage and feeling free as a woman perhaps for the first time, it was not long before I embarked on a deep and passionate love affair with my soulmate, the man who passed away and who I have mentioned before. I was not aware of it yet, but by choosing partly unavailable men who were at some level destined to disappoint me, I was, in fact, living out of a story or a belief system in which true love is unobtainable. This is the tragic side of Aphrodite whose constant search for love (often in the wrong areas) leaves her old, bitter and lonely. As Landau states, *"Women who embody the Aphrodite archetype have much less choice in how they react or behave than they, or others imagine."*[5] She is compelled to follow the spark of Eros no matter what, often throwing caution to the winds and entering doomed if at first, enticing love affairs. She may end up being left rejected and abandoned when the relationship ends. Landau continues, *"The dark side of the pursuit of beauty is especially apparent with aging, when the Aphrodite woman must become something other than a source of beauty or dwindle to a lonely and bitter end."*

Living Out of Stories

Although we are influenced by archetypal and universal images, we are also simultaneously creating our own stories. On a spiritual level, I believe that we are co-creators in our life. This means that we create a story and that we live out of that story; stories that our soul carries with us into this incarnation; stories that come alive at night in our dreams when sleep encourages their emergence out of where they lie, hidden in the unconscious. Our inner drama – our story – is also an expression of how we have chosen to live out our soul contract, so that we will be drawn to those that express particular challenges we have to face and lessons we have to learn. Relationships, and love relationships in particular, bring out and activate our stories, which is why they offer us the greatest opportunities for soul growth. The archetype comes closer and takes more human form as it were, through our early life experiences. Often, our inner drama is reflected in a favourite fairy tale that was read to us in childhood. Fairy stories often underpin a person's psychological make-up. These stories will have a particular resonance in their soul. In people that can recall them, there is usually an intensive relationship between a particular tale and that child's psychological development. Children identify with different figures in the fairy tale, so that the tales can be a bridge to the unconscious. This happens during the developmental stage in childhood, when the archetypal and mythical imagery is close to the child. Fairy-tale figures are usually personifications of a person's unconscious complexes. Identifying with stories, along with their experiences, is how children learn about life, about its struggles and its joys, and the rewards for the successful accomplishment of life tasks.[6]

Why is a child drawn to a particular tale? There is something in the child's soul contract and early life experience that finds resonance in the fairy tale. *Rapunzel* and *The Little Mermaid*, for example, are tales of attempted development of the female ego out of the dominance of the mother archetype. Both heroines are in search of their counterparts, their animus or masculine sides. Union with their inner man creates wholeness and allows them to come into psychological consciousness, and also to relate to an outer man. In the foreground of the fairy-tale plot of both those stories is a yearning to connect with the masculine, personified by the prince. In *The Little Mermaid*, there is furthermore a failed attempt at a love relationship, due in no small part to the girl's inability to verbally express her feelings. The Little Mermaid needs human legs in order to have a chance with her beloved prince. Feet and legs represent our standpoint in life, our ability to assert ourselves and establish a relationship to reality. But the price is too much for the mermaid to bear, for in exchanging her voice for human legs, she loses her ability to communicate her feelings, and thus her chance to find true love.

Particular fairy tales, like archetypes, can play a big part in a person's life, as I was to realise myself. At the end of our first year in psychotherapy training our tutor gave us an assignment. When I was told we were to write a 5,000-word essay and hand it in by the last day of term, I grumbled and protested. However, when the assignment was explained to us, I perked up considerably. My interest had been stimulated; we were to pick a fairy story (or myth) of our choice and write an interpretation of it from three different psychoanalytical perspectives: the Freudian, Jungian and Kleinian. It was an interesting and challenging task, and one I enjoyed, particularly because, along with most of my colleagues new to this way of thinking, we were more or less unaware of how this would reveal our own inner worlds. By our choice of tale, we unconsciously revealed ourselves! I am still amused when I think about how myself, along with my unsuspecting friends and college mates, poured our intimate stories out on paper, thinking we were merely exposing how much theoretical material we had retained throughout the year! We never suspected that into our renditions we had put our own soul's story, thus revealing much more than we intended. In actual fact, our choice of fairy story or myth was not really a choice. Nudged by our unconscious, we were compelled to reveal and repeat our own inner dramas through the stories we wrote about and interpreted.

"She said that she would dance with me if I brought her red roses," cried the young student, *"but in all my garden there is no red rose."* Oscar Wilde's *The Nightingale and the Rose* depicts the yearning for love and a failed attempt at finding it. It is no surprise that this was my chosen fairy tale! The story of *The Nightingale and the Rose* is about unobtainable or unavailable love, since the young Prince is not prepared to give of himself and open his heart.[7] Despite the nightingale's terrible sacrifice which results in a beautiful red rose blooming in his garden, the Prince, in his cold-heartedness, discards and rejects true love. Wilde's poignant tale carries another important element, common in many relationships; the notion of sacrificing oneself for the other. There are many lovers who enter a relationship with someone who is wounded or who cannot love them, because they are drawn by the challenge. "I'll change him," turns into, "I'll love him so much, I'll help him open his heart," or "I'll save him". These are words that some women think about when such a dynamic is present in their love relationships. Men also

can be drawn to love a woman they perceive as wounded and unable to love. And from what I have learnt from life and from my Jungian work in particular, a wounded 'anima' man is often drawn to an equally wounded woman or lover. An 'anima' man is a term I use to describe a man whose connection to his 'inner woman' – his heart – is not solid, usually because he has not as yet successfully negotiated his mother complex. He will then experience his anima purely through projection, onto his partner or lover. In layman's terms, it seems to be that lovers often attract each other directly from their soul's promptings. I believe that what happens is that our soul guides us towards people and experiences that will best serve it. If your soul's journey is to learn about love, you may learn about it through your love relationships. There is a healing dimension that is usually activated in a love affair, no matter how it turns out, even for the Aphrodite woman if she is willing to learn from her 'failed' relationships.

I straighten in my chair, the Goddess appears again and gently takes the pen from my hand. She nods towards the cave's entrance and indicates we should take a walk and explore the vast, warm waters of the seabed. There is much to be discovered in the deepest depths of the ocean, a vast beautiful world of new, as yet undiscovered life. Soon I am swimming and basking in the warm turquoise waters.

Chapter Four

The Blue Room

Called by the spirit of the sea, I enter the ocean and allow myself to sink down through its multicoloured depths. As I descend, the waters became colder and darker before gradually turning warm, bright and welcoming. Soon I can feel my feet land on warm sand and I stretch my toes, relishing the grainy softness under my bare feet and the warm water that seems to caress and embrace me. At the bottom of the sea I find the Blue Room. Its entrance is through the deck of an abandoned, ancient shipwreck. Away in the distance I had seen the dark spires of the wreck jut out from a long greenish shape that appeared to be lying on its side. Curious, I approach, somewhat cautiously. As I near, a bright blue light appears and guides me so that very soon I am on the wreck and entering a beautiful Blue Room inside which sit an old man and woman. Dressed in dark blue robes with silver stars that sparkle as they move, I know instinctively that they are wise soulful beings. They beckon me in. As I approach I see that although they appear old, they emanate a timeless, ageless majesty. They are seated side by side and so close they almost appear as one. I feel a sense of deep love, serenity and oneness. They smile and welcome me. The woman indicates I should sit and directs me to a large, padded seat covered in the same rich blue and silver fabric as their clothes. I am sitting, and again as before, an ornate, beautiful desk appears on which are several quills and pens. On the desk also are a set of wooden 'lovebirds' which seem to be sculpted from a light brown gold-coloured bog wood; they loom over me as I sit and appear as protective, benevolent forces. "Write about Love and Relationships; write about the Inner Marriage," the couple urge. I take up one of the quills and write. Soon the Blue Room fades and I am walking on the shoreline by the sea again.

The Fire of Love

The minute I heard my first love story
I started looking for you, not knowing
How blind that was.
Lovers don't finally meet somewhere
They're in each other all along.
– Rumi

Love has a numinous energy that calls us. Most, if not all of us hope that we can find another soul to love, a companion to share our human journey. Love relationships offer us a unique opportunity to grow. From personal experience and from my many years as a therapist, I know our love relationships form an integral part of our spiritual journey. As such, through enduring, sometimes suffering and often simply experiencing great happiness and fulfilment as well as the ups and downs of relating in love, we journey towards emotional maturity and spiritual evolution. Loving, and relating, is fundamental to our spiritual growth. The consciousness of relating to another being opens us to union and wholeness that is not possible any other way. It is only through the constant chaffing of differences that we learn to deal with 'otherness'. Through this acceptance we move to inner wholeness. Paradoxically too, by relating and getting to know 'the other' we further our own self-awareness and get to know ourselves, and how we are and behave in relationships.

The search for love and the inner marriage is archetypal and deeply engrained in our souls. I can truly say I have walked and continue to walk that path. In my early forties, I left the UK and returned to my native Ireland to start a new life with two of my children. This was not something I did lightly. The move coincided with the death of my second marriage. Although sudden when the final 'betrayal' came, it had been a slow agonising death and one I had resisted, even though part of me knew this marriage had to end. Nonetheless, although nursing a badly broken heart and a latent depression, I was determined to make a good life in a place I considered 'home'. I had qualified a few years previously as a psychoanalytical psychotherapist and my first book was in the final stages of being written and published. As a card carrying practical Capricorn I had put feelers out ahead of my departure from the UK so that I already had work lined up when I arrived back in Ireland. I soon set up a busy psychotherapy practice in Dublin. I was also at that time tutor and supervisor on several psychotherapy trainings, all of which kept me very busy. The first year and a half were dark and difficult, I was struggling with the sense of betrayal and abandonment at the ending of my marriage; I lived for work and my children. I did not socialise much and didn't engage in any relationships. Eventually as life follows death, I slowly healed myself and emerged stronger and more resilient, and more importantly, I emerged with a deeper sense of who I was and a firm trust in the universe and life itself.

Then I met my soulmate and a great fire was lit in my heart. There followed a tumultuous four and a half years in which I experienced a lifetime. There was love, deep love, profound joy, pain, separation, tugging and resistance, hurt and abandonment. There was also a great sense of fun, of life and of, unbelievable as this may sound, lightness of being. My late partner was a humorous, creative man, full of the joys of life, which sadly masked a deeply hurt heart and a bruised soul. We not only embarked on a love affair but on a creative endeavour connected with my work. My late partner was a gifted graphic designer crafting the cover of my first book and a lot more. Even though after some years we parted, and not well, my relationship with him drove me straight to the door of unconditional love. And to a profound spiritual awakening. I include our story here because I know I have him to thank for the precious experience of awakening to true unconditional love. The intensity of my love for him had a divine quality to it and propelled me onwards to pursue my soul's calling. It was as though a doorway was opened in me from my heart straight to God. The sheer intensity of love that I felt was greater than I have ever experienced before and probably since. There was a luminous and numinous quality to this love, that is how strong it was. Our soul connection and relationship was a huge heart opening and spiritual awakening for me. It remains with me still and has informed and enriched my life as I continue my earthly journey without him.

Heartbreak as a Spiritual Opening

As already written, I have experienced heartbreak many times and several lost loves. My last book *Love in a Time of Broken Heart* was written after the ending of perhaps my most profound love relationship – the one I refer to above. The break-up shook me to my roots. When my former partner and I broke up I felt I had jumped from the highest cliff down into the depths of the sea. I floundered in those depths, lost and adrift, for some time. Loving and losing the man whom I believed was my soulmate, and with whom I thought I was destined to be with for the rest of my life, propelled me into a deep and profound soul journey. Instead of ink, that book was written with my tears, both of sorrow and of joy. What started out as a journey to heal my heart ended up opening many new and wonderful doors to understanding heartbreak, soul connections, and the enduring and eternal nature of love. *Love in a Time* is testimony to my own journey through heartbreak to healing and love. Devasted after the break-up, I entered the darkness of my soul, and in time, discovered a world more beautiful than I ever imagined. At the time, if there was a message I wanted to convey in the book, it was that we can find happiness and love if we go within and follow the path that heartbreak opens for us.

Just one year after my book was published, my soulmate and former partner passed away. And although we were not together when he died, we had been in touch just shortly beforehand, since, as is common with profound soul connections, we were never far from each other's thoughts and hearts. More poignantly, our deep and enduring love was only fully acknowledged by him as he was nearing the end of his earthly journey. As a deeply wounded man he had never been able to fully acknowledge his love for me whilst we were together. Such was our connection, he was able to call out to me in spirit just before he finally left the planet. And I was able to hear him. Unaware of either his short illness or the fact he was nearing death, for some days before he passed away I had experienced a disturbing sense of 'doom'. This prescience had no particular direction or object, I just felt an impending sense of catastrophe which I didn't understand. I realised after the event that my soul was 'tuning' in to him and meeting his call in his final hours. The experience profoundly affected me and rooted in me a firm belief in the power of our ability to connect energetically with all life on different planes and the psyche's immense capabilities. It also confirmed what I had already intuited, that soul connections are strong and powerful and carry a numinous energy, and that love transgresses boundaries. I recall that for several days I could not shake off this sense of impending doom; it affected me in the cells of my body. Such is the power of energy. Since that time, more than ten years ago now, I have never again truly doubted my intuition, the power of my soul or the beauty of soul connections, and mostly, the enduring and eternal nature of love.

His unexpected death again shook me deeply and tore at the roots of our profound soul connection, leaving me dangling and rootless. It felt as though I had been cut adrift, one half of a whole that had shattered. It took me some time to heal from his death. I had help from several places, including the shamans and healers I met whilst I was training in traditional and herbal medicine in Mexico. I had gone there a few weeks after he died, so my wound was still fresh, as was noted quickly by the shamans and healers present. And although I thought that, as a therapist and 'healer' myself, I knew all about mourning and healing my heart, I soon learnt that in effect, I had arrived in Mexico with a firmly closed heart chakra. "Estas de luto" (you are in mourning), I was soon told as they beckoned me to their healing rooms to perform some of their shamanic rituals. Their work with me released much needed tears from my overburdened heart and shattered soul. I will always remember with gratitude and love my time in Mexico learning about 'Curanderismo' and herbal medicine. And as for my love and soulmate, he still comes to me in my dreams – I feel he is always with me. He has taken up position in my psyche as the lover archetype and my teacher on love so that when he appears, it is usually to help me.

Being in love and suffering the loss of love throws us into a deep place. Our hearts are touched and we open ourselves to depths of pain and joy, to profound feeling perhaps never experienced before. Though we are all probably destined at some stage to have our hearts broken, it is less often understood that this 'break' enables us to 'open' our hearts more. And that this opening is to the Divine, to infinite love. There is a Sufi prayer that asks God to, "Shatter my heart so a new room can be created for a Limitless Love." A shattered heart opens itself to its expansion. Experiencing the loss of love, paradoxically, returns us to love, to the inner marriage, and to the sacred wisdom of the heart. I have found that in profound vulnerability, a deeper intelligence comes through. Heartbreak in this sense is a sacred initiation. The journey to healing after heartbreak is well documented in great myths and stories handed down to us as part of our archetypal heritage. The voyage always involves trials and tests, death (of the ego) and rebirth – new life. Part of this journey involves the willingness to suffer, and to be in exile for a while. Symbolically, we are in exile anyway because when we are broken-hearted we are divided, and our search to return home to ourselves represents our healing journey. To be an exile is to be apart from others, divided within, and forced into a search for belonging. We have to endure the dark night of the soul. The dark night is like death in that everything we know is dissolved. Our castles are destroyed and our troops are killed. The battle has been fought and lost. Our dreams are smashed and our hopes are dashed. And our old heart has to die along with the relationship that is no longer.[8]

Deeper than the Sea: Encountering the Inner Marriage

Just as at the start of this chapter I write about encountering the old wise man and woman, personifications of the divine inner marriage during a meditation, an experience of heartbreak can equally take you to this encounter. Often, the journey to heal your heart will bring you to a dark night in which you will be forced to go inwards. When life on the outside fails to bring you the solace you need, you will be forced to go within and listen to your soul and to the voice of your psyche. A call you may have ignored until now. Answering that call will hold many rewards for you, for although you are in despair, your psyche shows you fresh potential, new life. What has been needing to birth in you has been waiting for this moment. And it may be that for some time your psyche speaks of your brokenness, but in time as you begin to surrender to your soul, images of union, love and wholeness will appear. Your psyche holds and can produce many images of healing and wholeness which you can access as you seek to heal your heart. But you need to be open to it. Heartbreak is one such time. You could say our hearts have been broken 'open' creating a doorway to divine love. When we are heartbroken we feel alone, cut off from love and separated from all that may be life affirming. In the anguish of our separation or sense of aloneness, we cry out for our 'other half' to feel whole again. An image of union and of wholeness such as of the divine inner marriage can help us towards healing our hearts. I have many such images both in my workroom and my bedroom, mostly pictures of sculptures and paintings by Rodin, Camille Claudel, Frida Kahlo and others. Bronze plaques with the words "the heart that loves is always young" by Oscar Wilde, pictures of Jung and a plaque at the entrance of my consulting room as Jung had with the words "Bidden or not bidden, God is present". Poetry, especially those of some of the mystics such as Rumi, one of the greatest love poets I know, Rilke, Pablo Neruda, Emily Dickinson and many more. Surrounding ourselves with such objects can be very healing for us and even activate our inner healer so that by just looking at the images or reading a few lines of poetry brings us solace and peace – and a sense of wholeness. Nature and living as I do by the sea also has a healing effect on our soul. Many people walk in nature as a sort of healing or therapy when they feel stressed, hurt or unsure.

One of the meditations and visualisations I use during my healing retreats and workshops involves going on a journey to both the bottom of the ocean and the top of a mountain. It is called deeper than the ocean, higher than the mountain. I use it as a guided visualisation to initiate participants to explore their unconscious as well as their spirituality, and crucially, their masculine and their feminine sides. From a soul psychology perspective, this visualisation is also about exploring the feminine/mother and the masculine/father energies in each person and the balance of both. It is a long visualisation that nearly always reveals a great deal to the person doing it. Individual unconscious imagery is spontaneously produced during the visualisation which can then be amplified through the process Jung called "active imagination". What is revealed can be powerful and hold a numinous energy which can be harnessed for that individual's healing. The symbolic meaning of journeying to the bottom of the ocean is manifold but generally the sea represents the unconscious, the feminine, the mother and womb life. Water also symbolises feeling and, of course, healing. Conversely, climbing the mountain can reveal our spiritual aspirations, the masculine aspect of us and the father energy. Entering the unconscious or going deep is a normal process of depth psychology and Jungian work in particular. Navigating the deep waters of the unconscious is an integral part of soul healing. In its depths we may encounter lost dreams, hurts, resentments and aspects of our soul we haven't yet discovered or brought into life. In the sea too, we may meet our feminine nature and how we might have experienced our mother and our very early life, pre- and post-natal.

I will return to this subject in the next chapter.

What is the Inner Marriage?

The inner marriage is about wholeness, union, oneness and love. Fundamentally, the inner marriage is about the balancing of the masculine and feminine within oneself. Carl Jung believed that every human being has contra-sexual components; in other words, all of us have masculine and feminine energies, and what every individual seeks is a balance between these two energies, in order to feel complete. In this respect, outer union with a partner is merely a reflection of our need for inner balance. Or, to put it another way, the drive to relate in love is merely the outer manifestation of the universal drive for wholeness and union within. That is the reason why, for so many of us, the urge to love another soul and have a partner is so strong. You could say that loving another soul leads us to experience the divine or, more accurately, our own pure whole natures. Jung suggested that the drive to wholeness is inherent to the psyche and is a process of gradual lifetime unfolding. Individuation is a natural process – an inner union that, in essence, is essential

to the spiritual well-being of every individual. The search
for inner wholeness is generally given expression in our love
relationships. Of the Inner Marriage the poets say:

> *When two souls have finally found each other there is established*
> *between them a union which begins on earth and continues forever*
> *in Heaven.*
> – Victor Hugo

The mystics say:

> *If you want to make progress on the path and ascend to the places*
> *you have longed for, the important thing is not to think much but*
> *to love much, and so do whatever best awakens you to love.*
> – St. Teresa of Ávila

The search for love is archetypal, ageless and universal. In some
deep part of our soul we all have a sense of love, as well as a
memory of wholeness, and of belonging. We also have a sense
of having lost this wholeness, and this further fuels our search
and our longing. Some psychologists would tell us that what
we are searching for is to return to the nirvana that we thought
we experienced when we were in our mothers' wombs. My own
belief is that while the birth experience is most definitely our first
great experience of physical separation, it is merely a reminder
of an earlier separation, and causes us to search endlessly for
the person who will give us the desired sense of completion.
Often this is a nameless yearning we feel in our hearts and we
imagine it will be healed through meeting the perfect partner,
our soulmate. Whether our search is for that 'other half' as Plato
calls it, or the one that will complete us and lead us to the divine
mystery, we all seek wholeness. Our innate sense of belonging
and of loss is thus archetypal and primeval. The fundamental
nature of our great myths is about the struggle to return to a

state of oneness. Whether this longing is expressed through the various world religions or spiritual traditions or simply in everyday life, they all lead us to the same place, a desire to return home.

Archetypal Imprint

I have experienced the archetypal imprint of the inner marriage in a very personal way. Love, and finding a soulmate and life partner to love, has been, for an Aphrodite woman with the sun in the seventh house, my life's quest. I was perhaps in my late thirties when I discovered just how deeply imprinted into my soul was the sense, yearning and search for the perfect union. During a difficult period in my marriage, I had consulted an astrologer. Always interested in astrology, I was curious to see what my 'stars' might be telling me and I hoped to get some guidance there. I still remember the day I went to my astrologer's South London flat for our consultation. We sat in her colourful living room, an older wise woman dressed in strong, vibrant colours surrounded by crystals and other artefacts; she seemed somehow familiar. I was sitting opposite her, on a grey spring day, when she spoke these words. *"I have cast your natal chart,"* she pointed to some drawings on the table and pronounced. *"At the time of your conception, your parents were perfectly balanced and in love – in other words, you have within you the imprint of the ultimate perfect union between the masculine and the feminine."* I stared at her, not understanding wholly the significance of her words but feeling their impact in my body. I resonated deep inside to her announcement. They felt true and real, but quite quickly the confusion started, and the questions. If I had this imprint, then why was I finding it so hard to find and have a stable, loving relationship? At this stage in my life I had already married and divorced once, and was into my second marriage. You could say I had no trouble attracting men and had no fear of embarking on the journey to love another soul, generally hurling myself headlong into relationships. But my restless soul and passionate nature would not rest easily – not until it seemed, I found the perfect partner!

It was some years (and relationships) later, along with further study and practice as a Jungian psychotherapist, before I fully realised the import of not just this meeting, but what it was that I was being told. I was searching to heal myself and to become more whole by balancing my inner feminine and masculine. I was searching for my own inner marriage. In essence, along with others called to heal this aspect of their soul, my journey was one of recovering inner wholeness. I would do this through relating to and loving many men. I would do this through living and experiencing several love relationships some of which would carry the energies I needed to deal with such as abandonment, betrayal and deceit. And although no one wants to experience heartbreak, abandonment, betrayal or deceit, if it is in the service of your soul, you may be guided to do so. I didn't know then what I have since come to know, that our relationships are in service to our soul and its sacred contract. Here I was, an Aphrodite woman, drawn to love, but at least this search now had a deeper meaning. It was a quest, a journey to heal my soul. I gained solace and a kind of peace from knowing this. In essence, this search, over time, would take me to great spiritual growth and transformation. It has taken me directly to my inner psyche and to connect with my soul's purpose.

Love has a transcendent and numinous quality that draws us and can take us straight to the Divine. And it is sometimes through loving (and perhaps losing) another person that we are thrust into a spiritual search so that our love relationships become an intimate part of our spiritual journey to reach the inner depths of our own souls. In short, as we search outwards for the person we believe will 'complete' us, we are simultaneously searching inwards for a sense of wholeness. In this sense, our love experiences become initiations of a sort. All initiations are spiritual tasks of empowerment that we can choose to either engage with or not. Love offers us the opportunity to heal a loss of connection with our souls and our inner life. Also, and more importantly, intimate love relationships offer us a unique opportunity to heal childhood wounds and overcome the scar tissue of our past. I remember my first analyst telling me, "You do your best work in relationships." I understood her to mean, at the time, that my sometimes tortuous and anguished recanting of the struggles in my heart, as I sought to love and be loved, had meaning for my psychological and spiritual growth. We learn a great deal in our relationships with others, and most especially love relationships. I am reminded of the words of one of my favourite poets: *"For one human being to love another: that is perhaps the most difficult of all our tasks, the ultimate, the last test and proof, the work for which all other work is but preparation."*[9] Yes.

The Long Journey to Love

It can take a long while and usually a lifetime to learn to truly love. Negotiating our love relationships and learning from them can be a long, sometimes tortuous journey. We may have to travel down many roads that lead to dead ends, negotiate difficult corners, kiss a lot of frogs and experience heartbreak, perhaps several times, before we feel whole enough in ourselves to love unconditionally or at least to know unconditional love. Love affairs offer us a unique opportunity to find out who we are, what we are, and what stories or belief systems we are still living out of. You will remember I wrote about this in the last chapter. I wrote about how we create our own stories and dramas and live out of them. We unconsciously create these stories, generally, but not uniquely as a reaction to our earliest experiences. These dramas or belief systems, such as "I am unlovable" or "unlucky in love," act like unconscious forces that inform our behaviour and push us along certain paths which may not be considered fruitful from an ego perspective but which can further our soul growth and learning. It might mean, for example, that we will be drawn towards certain people and relationships that are not 'good' for us or that are destined to disappoint or hurt us in some way. We don't always choose the 'right' people to love! There are many reasons for this, a lot of which has to do with our early life experience. Since the first relationship we have is with our parents, a template is created in our psyche based on them. So, even though at a conscious level we may say we will not marry someone like our mother or father, we often do! Our lived experience of our parents creates inner images in our psyche that inform us. Our mother for example will become our inner feminine and our masculine will have the face of our father. Usually, we choose principal actors that fit into our life script. By this I mean that we unconsciously choose who we will fall in love with and with whom we will have relationships. We do this because we want to grow, heal and learn. Our soul will draw people into our life that will best serve its need to evolve. So if at a soul level, our contract is to learn how to overcome abandonment, guess what? We will (unconsciously) choose the best person to do this even though obviously, at a personality level, it is not our wish to be abandoned. However, the growth process involved in navigating such a situation will serve our spiritual evolution. Ultimately, relationships serve the soul.

My Journey to Love

When I started my own journey towards healing I spent some years in Jungian therapy. My first therapist, an analytical psychologist trained in Zurich, became both a wise woman and earth mother to me. We travelled down many roads, some very difficult, and entered many rooms in my psyche I had not even known existed. There was crying, laughing and a lot of trekking into the inner terrain of my soul. I suffered, I endured, I discovered and I wrote. My analyst encouraged me to write and I did, reams and reams of it. Writing was my medium, she told me. I loved her deeply and was devasted when she left to go back to her native USA after some three years working together. Nonetheless, our work left me more rounded and whole than when I had started, and with shelves of note and dream books. Through her I discovered how much I had felt abandoned in my early life and most especially when I was born and separated from my mother for an extended time due to my prematurity. I learnt that bonding was not something I had experienced and how our earliest relationship experiences can affect how we relate in later life. My first book *Songs from the Womb: Healing the Wounded Mother*, written around this time, bears testimony to my own journey but also to that of many others and to the teachings and research in the field of pre- and perinatal psychology. Birth and life in the womb are formative soul experiences creating patterns we carry with us into later life. The book is based on my experience as a birth teacher, therapist and mother, and addresses the 'loss of soul' encountered by many due to our modern medicalised way of birth which strips nature of its spiritual dimension.

I will return to this important topic later in the book.

I knew at a profound level how much my birth in extremely difficult circumstances and my prenatal life had affected me in creating imprints which would later resurface. I found being openly vulnerable and negotiating intimacy in a close relationship did not come easily to me. "You are like an empty ocean," my therapist told me one day. I was hungry for love and had certainly not learnt to love myself. I learnt how a sense of abandonment was my biggest wound and so vast was this wound it could take a lifetime to heal my heart. My writing helped me as did our work with my dreams. Jungians usually but not uniquely work with dreams. An avid dreamer, I would diligently write them up in my dream book and bring them to our therapy sessions. During this time too, my latent psychic intuitive energies began to make themselves felt. I would often dream of what was yet to come for me along the journey, and had many visitations from guides and ancestors with messages designed to help me become more conscious. Deciphering and understanding the symbolic meaning of my dreams I left to her. I did the feeling, the journeying and the writing. I was still a young woman; I entered analysis when I was thirty years old and pregnant with my third child. Having completed a training in dance and drama therapy the previous year I had been guided to seek more personal work. A senior Jungian analyst on the course had encouraged me. And although I had a busy life as a wife and mother and a strong energetic persona, I discovered I also had a passionate nature that felt very deeply but that I had never really expressed. I had difficulty showing my vulnerability and tended to protect people from my tears and pain. I presented a strong capable persona. Deeply buried in my heart was my love wound and deeper still my unconsciously held belief that I would always be abandoned. I believe that my twice weekly sessions with my therapist at this time were a lifesaver in helping me become who I really was and discover a hitherto unknown but vital part of myself.

I pause to look at the beautiful carved 'lovebirds' on my desk and am back in the Blue Room again. My companions signal that we should leave the room now and take a walk further out into the sea. There is much buried in the ocean, and many treasures and gifts to be discovered.

Chapter Five

Deeper than the Sea: Exploring the Depths of Your Soul

Far out into the sea, the water is as blue as the petals of the most
beautiful cornflower, and as clear as the purest glass.
But it is very deep, deeper than any cable will sound;
many steeples must be placed one above the other
to reach from the ground to the surface of the water.
And down there live the sea people.
– From *The Little Mermaid*

Like all children, I loved stories. There was no story that fascinated and touched me as much as *The Little Mermaid*. I would make my aunt read it to me over and over again, and I can still see the sad pictures in my mind of the Little Mermaid holding in her arms the unconscious prince she loved so much but could never have, the shipwreck, the sea witch and other scenes. I remember feeling the pain of the Little Mermaid as she took one step after another, on legs that felt as though a hundred sharp knives were piercing her. It seemed to me, then, that a terrible price was to be paid to win the heart of a mortal man, and that love was surely out of reach. I cried bitter tears for the Little Mermaid, for whom love seemed unobtainable, and I remember something lament deep inside me, and a resonance in my deepest being. The tale of the Little Mermaid had an impact on me at that time which, only now as an adult woman, I have fully understood. Was I destined to grapple with love, with finding my soulmate and life partner? Is part of my sacred contract to learn about love and the wisdom of the heart through relationships, and the search for a true soulmate? What is sure is that this story resonating, as it did at a deep level within me, revealed a lot about my feminine heart and soul, and perhaps about my life's journey.

Travelling the long road to love and spiritual well-being will mean trekking our souls. It means travelling to the bottom of the sea, it means digging our psyche for our archetypes and what we may unconsciously be carrying in the form of energetic and psychological imprints. It means having the courage to dive deep and be prepared to painstakingly unravel the knots that might be holding us back from fully flowing with our life. For the soul is deep and mysterious and knows no bounds. The sea is a potent metaphor for the unconscious and so exploring her depths is where we will find aspects of ourselves deeply buried. In there too we can uncover our earliest wounds and experiences that have left a mark on our soul.

The Roots of the Soul

Our birth is but a sleep and a forgetting;
The Soul that rises with us, our life's Star,
Hath had elsewhere its setting
And cometh from afar;
Not in entire forgetfulness,
And not in utter nakedness,
But trailing clouds of glory do we come
From God, who is our home
– Wordsworth

When do we begin? My inherent knowing is that birth into physical life is merely just that, and that our soul, our spirit, our essence exists outside of this event and 'comes from afar'. I believe that our soul is eternal and that we take on many different 'life' mantles and embodiments in different lifetimes in the service of our soul's growth. Reincarnation is less of a belief to me than a deep knowing. I have always had a sense of being that transcends this particular lifetime. In the same way that our wounds are conduits to our healing, each lifetime lived is an opportunity to learn spiritual lessons in the service of our soul's contract. There is part of us made of eternal starlight and it is this very spark we need to connect with in order to heal. As already said, we have in part a divine nature that sparkles and shines through if we allow it to. It is the divine in us that connects us with infinite love and abundance. When we feel part of this sense of oneness, we are able to enlist it to help us heal our lives. Our higher selves or the Jungian Self with a big S are other words to describe the divine part of us which encompasses all that we truly are or can be.

Our roots go a long way back. Studies and research in the fields of consciousness and pre- and perinatal psychology suggest not only that birth and prenatal life are formative experiences affecting later life, but that such memories can be recovered. This awareness led me to further explore the roots of human experience. I see life as a continuum and the soul or 'spirit' of each person as eternal. What we now know about the infinite nature of human consciousness has necessitated a shift in belief structures. Whereas formerly, it was generally thought that consciousness was created by and limited to the human brain, now it is seen as something that exists outside and independent of us, although we form part of it. Consciousness in its essence is not bound to matter and the human psyche has no boundaries or limits. Psychiatrist and author Stanislav Grof, pioneer in transpersonal psychology, wrote some time back that,

> If we accept the expanded view of consciousness, it means accepting also that our lives are not shaped only by the immediate environmental influences since the day of our birth but, of at least equal importance, they are shaped by ancestral, cultural, spiritual and cosmic influences beyond

the scope of what we can perceive with our physical senses.

Ongoing scientific discoveries and new paradigms mean that an increasingly broad image of the psyche exists, together with an acceptance of its capability for expanded and higher consciousness.

Such an extended view of the human psyche was fully accepted by Carl Jung. In *Seven Sermons of the Dead*, first published in 1916, Jung describes transpersonal experiences which were to deeply influence his work. There, he began communicating with a spirit being who called himself *Philemon*. In his observations about the workings and scope of the human psyche, Jung concluded that Philemon had taught him about the reality of the psyche as an objective fact. Later work and notably *The Red Book* have placed Jung as both a visionary and pioneer in many ways. He expounded the ability of the psyche to record and remember experiences which went far beyond the confines of biography through his concepts of the collective unconscious and the existence of archetypes which informed our minds and governed our behaviour. Archetypes are universal forces, or sources of energy that exist in their own right and that influence mankind. We are all influenced by our ancestral heritage for example, often living forwards or onwards the unlived life of our parents or grandparents and even those that have 'gone before'.

It is more than twenty years since I wrote and published *Songs from the Womb* – a book which broadly speaking placed birth and life in the womb as formative experiences that inform our later life. *Songs from the Womb* also looks at birth as a Soul Experience that far transcends the medical view of birth as a physical event. Groundbreaking at the time, it was said to demolish one of the most pervasive myths of our time, namely that birth was a physical event to be managed by doctors. Quoting from the press release at the time, *"Birth is an experience which is deeply engraved in our souls, leaving traces that permeate our lives. Anchoring her insights in Jungian psychology, Benig Mauger highlights the 'loss of soul' many feel as a result of our modern medicalised way of birth where technology has replaced nature."* At that time, working with pregnant and post-natal women at the holistic birth centre I had created, I was acutely aware of the negative psychological effects endured by women (and their babies) during traumatic birth experiences. Indeed, it was largely this awareness that led me to further train in traditional psychoanalytic psychotherapy and guided my studies and research in pre- and perinatal psychology. Above all, the knowledge I gained at this time, of prenatal life and birth being such a formative event creating patterns we carry with us into later life, and of the pain, scarring and suffering sustained by women and their babies during a traumatic birth, led me directly on the path of healing. Healing ourselves of these soul scars from our earliest life felt essential if we were to be psychologically and physically well. At the same time, I was acutely aware of the desire to guide others to a healing path and to help women create empowering and fulfilling birth experiences. That was my motivation in setting up and running my holistic birth centre in the late eighties-early nineties.

Soul Waves

"The story of those who have gone before continues to unfold in us," writes Jung. Some years after *Songs from the Womb*, I gave a presentation at an international conference marking new psychological paradigms. Entitled Soul Waves, it looked at how psychological patterns are formed and how familial and archetypal imagery gets transmitted from generation to generation. Researchers and professionals both in the field of psychology and consciousness were asking questions to ascertain where 'consciousness' in the human psyche may begin. How are we influenced by our family and cultural

legacies? How are trans-generational patterns passed on from parent to child? How is it that a daughter often unconsciously carries her mother's, even her grandmother's wounds, thoughts, expectations, disappointments and pain? How does a son come to give birth to his father's unlived dreams? Incorporating the pre- and perinatal dimension of human life, I outlined a possible answer to these questions by way also of an explanation of the clinical material presenting at that time in my consulting room.

From a spiritual perspective, the soul's journey does not end in one lifetime. Life is a continuum, and our soul's existence may span many embodiments. We choose our embodiments in line with our spiritual challenges. This means that a soul wishing to incarnate will seek out the particular parents and circumstances that will offer it the greatest opportunities for growth. We are born into and inherit our chosen family's history and the myths of that time. This we call our personal and archetypal heritage. Each child is born with the contours of its life already present in potential. This means that we are born with and carry memories of both our ancestry and our future destiny. Our archetypal heritage and our soul's choices will inform how we go on to live our lives. We are all on an archetypal journey, and our soul contract ensures that we meet the right people and experience the right experiences, in order to fulfil our soul's purpose. This means that 'consciousness' in the form of energetic patterns and psychic imagery is passed on to us via our ancestral line.

There are many levels to this. Pre- and perinatal psychological work tells us that some of this heritage becomes 'activated' in the womb and begins to take shape. As the unborn child begins to experience life, his archetypal legacy begins to be humanised. In the womb, psyche begins to inform matter, and at birth, a child emerges, the product of his parents with the contours of his life already in place. Contrary to formal (early) orthodox psychoanalytic thought, man is not born a 'Tabula Rasa' (blank slate); he is born with the contours of his life already present in potential. His archetypal heritage ensures this. Jung describes it thus:

> *Man possesses many things which he has never acquired but has inherited from his ancestors. He is not born a 'tabula rasa' he is merely born unconscious. But he brings with him systems that are organised and ready to function in a specifically human way, and these he owes to millions of years of human development. Just as the migratory and nest-building instincts of birds were never learnt or acquired individually, man brings with him at birth the ground plan of his nature, and not only of his individual nature but of his collective nature. These inherited systems correspond to the human situations that have existed since primeval times: youth and old age, birth and death, sons and daughters, fathers and mothers, mating and so on. I have called this congenital and pre-existent instinctual model, or pattern of behaviour, the archetype.*[10]

Medicine and more specifically those who have studied the prenatal period of development confirm that a baby develops from foetus to child in an organised way. I will always remember sitting in the audience at a conference, maybe twenty years ago now, and listening to Obstetrician and Scientist Peter Nathanielsz talk about foetal life and how a growing baby is affected by his or her womb environment. Information not new to me, it was nonetheless the precision of the description of foetal life that drew my attention then. I knew that my mother had suffered frequent bleeds (haemorrhages) during her pregnancy with me before the emergency caesarean that resulted in my premature birth at seven months gestation. I was instantly thrown back to a time I didn't consciously remember and yet felt somewhere in the cells of my body. This bleeding would have affected me in several ways, frequent lack of oxygen the most obvious – it all made sense, my weak or 'thrifty' liver, my intestinal immaturity and so on. Foetal life, Nathanielsz went on to say, develops according to a finely tuned intelligent timed plan. "We know now that the foetus develops according to a finely tuned program. Life before birth progresses precisely and deliberately from one stage to the next according to a clear plan." Author of *Life Before Birth: The Challenges of Fetal Development*, Nathanielsz contends that at birth, the child is already an accomplished individual who has met and overcome numerous challenges during his development. An interesting finding is that the foetus will protect its brain at all costs, and so if there are adverse conditions which are likely to inhibit growth in the womb, it will deprive other organs in order to keep the brain oxygenated. This made me smile as I thought about how I have always had a good brain! And in many ways have used it to get by in times of emotional hardship. A sensitive child, school was only bearable to me because I loved learning. I often escaped into my head when things were difficult for me emotionally. This piece of self-awareness became very relevant during my own healing journey. As a therapist, however, I usually ask about a client's early life and include the circumstances of their birth, if possible. I ask about their mother's pregnancy with them, and the physical and emotional environment present at the time. All this information is highly relevant and can throw light on some of the formative influences in a person's life.

Humanising the Archetypes

When in 2004 I published *Reclaiming Father*, I was concerned with the role of the father in the early life of his child. *Songs from the Womb* gave mothers and the birthing experience front of place in a child's life; *Reclaiming Father*,[11] in outlining the formative influence of the Father, completed the picture. It is in this context that I presented Soul Waves and the contention that a child is already born with an archetypal inheritance to experience life in a particular way. So, a child is born knowing.

He knows about many things. Even if there is no father actively present for example, the child will have some kind of inner knowing about fathers and he will feel a lack. He may not be aware of what is lacking, but unconsciously he will try and find ways to fill it. He will draw on other things and people to clothe a skeleton father. You could say that the archetype is a skeleton waiting to be given flesh and is drawn into human life and activated through experience. In other words, life experience clothes and gives form to the archetype. In this way the father archetype, for example, is humanised through the personal father. So, the child learns about the father, he learns what this dim or indistinct feeling of father is through his experience of relating to his own father. This is what we mean when we talk about humanising the archetype. All of us need to have the archetype of the mother and the father humanised and embodied in our own parents in order to feel our way into life as secure human beings. The less a mother or father is 'present' to humanise the archetype for us, the more influence the (disembodied) archetype will have on our psyches, making it harder for us to incarnate as human beings.

Songs from the Womb was perhaps the first book of its kind in drawing together pre- and perinatal with Jungian psychology. Most Jungians stayed away from the 'baby' or very early life material, and most in the field of pre- and perinatal psychology did not take a Jungian or transpersonal view. At that time, I had just completed my training in an eclectic mix of psychoanalytic theories which heavily relied on Freud, Klein and Winnicott and which gave little time to the transpersonal element of human existence. But for me, the two fitted perfectly since my own experience both personally and as a clinician bore such a marriage out. The (Jungian) archetypal dimension can also be seen as the spiritual dimension. Jungian psychology is of course a transpersonal soul psychology and blends in well with the spiritual element necessary for healing. I believe the archetypal level of experience constitutes the roots of our experience. In the womb the archetypes become humanised. An unborn child will learn about life as her mother in particular experiences it. Her experiences in the womb will begin to flesh out her archetypal heritage and she will be marked by her intrauterine experience in such a way that unconsciously she will carry this experience into later life. Uncovering all of these imprints means entering the metaphorical sea of the unconscious and spending time there.

Chakras: The Energetic Connection

Then we come to the all-important energetic connection. Every human (and living thing) is known to possess an 'aura', an energy field. Additionally, there are central energy centres known as chakras. What is so fascinating is that we find that the chakra system is in actual fact an archetypal depiction of individual maturation through seven distinct stages. The first or root chakra, as already stated, refers to our prenatal lives and birth. In spiritual empowerment terms the root chakra represents tribal power – birth into our family of origin. It represents group archetypal identity. With difficult birth experience we can have root chakra imbalances since the Muladhara represents our foundation. On the human body, this chakra sits at the base of the spine and gives us the feeling of being grounded. When the root chakra is open, we feel confident in our ability to withstand challenges and stand on our own two feet. When it's blocked, we feel threatened, as if we're standing on unstable ground. There may also be fears relating to physical survival and emotional and material security. The root chakra represents the foundation of emotional and mental health. Psychologically, emotional and mental stability originate in the family unit and early social environment. My later learning further establishes the connection between the root chakra and both the immune and adrenal systems. When we don't feel safe, we enter a fight or flight response. Designed to sniff out danger, this response when overused can cause us to feel depleted and even sick. In my own life I have had to work hard to overcome a basic sense of being 'unsafe' which I believe dates back to my earliest life and difficult birth. Energetically, I work to bring light into my base chakra and repeat life-affirming phrases such as, "I am safe, I am held in the arms of the Earth Mother." Additionally, focusing on the colour red, walks in nature and bodywork such as yoga can be very helpful to balance our root chakra.

The sacral chakra, located in the lower abdomen, helps inform how we relate to our emotions. Our relationship chakra, it governs creativity and sexuality. There again, energetic imprints from our earliest relationship with our parents and siblings will inform this chakra. A blocked sacral chakra can translate as relationship, especially intimate relationship difficulties and a sense of feeling a lack of control over our life. There again, focusing on the colour orange, bringing light into the chakra and focusing on mantras such as, "I honour others and myself," may all be part of healing the sacral chakra. It must be noted, however, that transient blockages in any of the chakras especially the lower ones will happen from time to time as we work through various layers of our emotional 'baggage'.

The third chakra, the solar plexus or Manipura, is about your relationship to yourself. It is responsible for your self-esteem, confidence and self-worth. Blockages or imbalances in your solar plexus chakra might manifest as not liking yourself, perfectionism, self-criticism and self-doubt. Again our childhood experiences perhaps of being shamed or ridiculed may lodge in us such feelings. And since most of us have childhood wounds, we often internalise these in our stomachs, affecting our third chakra. Unrecognised feelings of shame or lack of self-worth usually surface here. The solar plexus chakra rules the pancreas and the digestive system. It is often said that our gut is our second brain, and gut health has now become a portal for wellness and healing. Needless to say, as already mentioned, with my sensitive digestive system I have had to really work hard to keep this chakra balanced. Since our solar plexus chakra is the epicentre of the mental body, it is here that we confront the judgments and beliefs that limit us. Focusing on the colour yellow and bringing in as much light as possible to my stomach, pancreas and digestive organs is a must for me, along with being mindful of the foods I eat and thoughts I have.

Next comes the all-important heart chakra or Anahata. The heart chakra is a bridge between the lower (materiality) and upper (spirituality) chakras. This chakra governs our ability to love and to be open to both give and receive love. If our heart chakra is blocked we will have difficulty opening up fully and experiencing deep compassion and empathy. A healing mantra such as, "I love myself and others unconditionally," focusing on the colour green and working on the issues that may be an obstacle to loving ourselves are all part of healing imbalances in the heart chakra. Once we have generated the self-love to open it, we are then ready to progress into the higher frequencies of the upper chakras. I have noted that feeling gratitude and giving thanks for even the little things in our life that bring us joy really opens the heart. Again, being so fortunate to live in nature and close to the sea, I do not miss a day of giving thanks for this joy. I see the animals grazing quietly in the field next to me, no matter the weather, and I feel gratitude to them for their steady, uncomplaining nature. I open the door of my kitchen every morning before I begin my day, to speak to the little birds who often come and feed off the small crumbs I leave out for them.

Moving to the Vishuddha chakra, located in the throat and governing our thyroid gland, this is the centre of communication and self-expression. It is from here that we speak our truth. The colour is light blue and the mantra can be, "I always speak my truth." As I experienced myself and wrote about earlier on in the book, when we have a blocked throat chakra we have trouble expressing and communicating our truth. Fears of doing so will be based on past experiences of not being accepted, being punished or ostracized for speaking out. A blocked or imbalanced throat chakra can express itself physically in many ways, sore throats, coughs and difficulty swallowing. When the spiritual energy and light is moving through us as we work through the lower chakras, we get closer to our authentic selves as beings of light. There may be fears about expressing our authenticity as spiritual beings for fear of not being accepted, or worse ostracized and punished. I know now that the burning sensation and physical symptoms I experienced as I was writing this book were a reflection of these deeply buried fears. Focusing on the colour blue, listening to music and self-expression all help open this chakra.

The third eye chakra controls our ability to see the bigger picture and connect with our intuition. It is from here that we receive messages from the divine and out of body beings such as spirit guides and celestial beings. This chakra is dark blue/purple and controls imagination, wisdom and intuition. The sight here is of what cannot be 'physically' seen but rather perceived or discerned – inner sight. In my own experience, we often block our third eye if we are trying to stop a flow of divine energy or information that might be coming in too fast. I certainly have felt this with resulting headaches and sinus congestion. On more than one occasion, I kept my third eye from opening because of fear. Fear of 'losing control' or going out of body or 'seeing' things I couldn't then communicate without fear of derision or worse. Focusing on the colour purple and bringing a lot of light into this chakra has helped me along with an increasing confidence in my ability to stay spiritually grounded while using my intuition and receiving intuitive guidance. Mantras such as, "I am open to receiving and exploring what cannot be seen," can also help, along with a trust in intuitive guidance.

The Sahasrara or crown chakra sits at the top of the head and represents our ability to be fully connected spiritually. When you open your crown chakra you are able to access higher consciousness. The colour is beautiful violet and speaks of our divine beauty as spiritual beings of light. Bringing in healing through this chakra is very powerful. Divine consciousness can not only heal our lives but can create miracles. However, it is important to always close the crown chakra after healing work and meditation so as to remain grounded in our everyday lives. While many of us have and will experience an opening of the seventh chakra, few people can sustain it long term. In my own life I have learnt now to trust enough to open my crown chakra to both receive healing and light, and to transmute negative or more dense energies I need to let go of. My mantras include, "I am a vessel for love and Divine light." Nonetheless, it takes time, experience, wisdom, and tremendous self-understanding to fully embody the interconnected nature of existence. And to accept all the suffering and injustices in the world. Knowing and experiencing ourselves as divine beings can't really be fully done until we have worked through our own, uniquely human wounds. This is why we need to trek our souls, to explore the depths of our own unconscious in a quest to heal ourselves of our wounds and become spiritually pure whilst remaining grounded in our human lives.

The Inside Story of Love Relationships

To go back to our relationships. There is always an 'inside story' going on which interacts with the outside so to speak. Having plunged into the sea and explored our earliest life imprints, we move sequentially to our love relationships. Two archetypes, that of the Anima and Animus, are really the architects of love and will direct our behaviour in relationships. For all of us, our first relationships create the template for later relationships – particularly relationships involving love and intimacy. Also, since our mothers and fathers are generally the first male and female in our lives, they make up our inner images of male and female and so influence our choice of partners later in life. Both men and women are greatly influenced by parental imagery; what they have internalised from their experience of their parents. If you have had a domineering mother for example, you will most likely have an inner image which tells you all women are domineering! If you have experienced an absent father you may have formed the (unconscious) idea that all men are unreliable or not likely to 'be there' for you. Trans-generational patterns are passed on in prenatal life since it is in the womb the archetypes become humanised and pre-existing trends or patterns begin to be activated. An archetype per se has no content, however, it is fleshed out and becomes embodied and made more 'real' through experience. The father archetype imprinted in the child becomes 'humanised' through his relationship with his actual father. The same goes for the mother. It is not that we are already primed to live a particular life or that our future is mapped out for us; it is more that we are predisposed to experience life a particular way. Our archetypal and psychic inheritance together with our early life experience greatly influence us, but need not determine how we go on to live our lives. We always have choice, but we generally need to become aware of our unconscious patterns before we can exercise this choice.

Nonetheless, both mother and father archetypes are very important and seminal to our development as men and women, and how they have been humanised for us will depend on our parents. The animus or inner masculine is responsible for our creativity, and more specifically, our ability to bring that creativity to life. Jung suggests the animus represents the spiritual aspect of the psyche in so far as this is as counterpart to nature, and a certain amount of this activated energy is necessary in order to become conscious. Ego consciousness involves a differentiation, a necessary break from nature. This means developing one's mental capabilities and the ability to see the bigger picture. In terms of creativity, the animus is responsible for the activation (or lack of activation) of that creativity in our lives. Developing the animus is important as a counterpart to the feminine. Developing the anima or feminine principle, which is more to do with relating, is also very important, because she represents everything to do with relationship, our relationship to ourselves, to others, to God, the world of love and emotions – how we relate in general. The anima in contrast to the animus, which is more about meaning than image, is always about relating, and in a man is usually about relating to a woman. This woman can be his inner woman or an outer woman who represents his anima. As Emma Jung writes:

> The anima figure, however, is characterised by the fact that all of its forms are at the same time forms of relationship. Even if the anima appears as priestess or witch, the figure is always in a special relationship to the man whose anima it embodies, so that it either initiates or bewitches him.[12]

Anima is intimately connected with love and relating.

Both men and women, all of us engaged in relationship, will be to a greater or lesser extent living and behaving out of the 'stories' from our past. Unaware of our part of the drama, we will undoubtedly project our unfinished or unresolved complexes onto our husbands/wives or lovers. We might dress our partner in the robes of a King and then wonder why they don't fit him. Or we might place our Goddess on a pedestal and then be dismayed when she topples and turns into an ordinary woman, complete with human flaws. We might find that the charm of our Peter Pan wears off when his frequent flights of fancy fail to bring in the bacon or pay the mortgage. Or tiring of the helplessness we initially found so appealing, our damsel in distress becomes, in actuality, Cruella de Vil, tying us to an unwanted responsibility. We wonder how all this can happen and how the dream of 'happy ever after' could have failed us so badly. We will continue to wonder, that is, until exhausted, we pull up the drawbridge to the outside world and start looking for the answers within ourselves. Looking within always produces results. We become more conscious when we rescue or recover lost parts of ourselves deep in our shadow. Our shadow buried in our unconscious also seeks to be known, just as we also seek wholeness. Unless each partner is willing to delve deeply into their own psyches and become more self-aware, the relationship flounders. It takes a lot of courage, strength, and a great deal of love and patience to heal from within. There is no other way. However, the idea that 'what we are seeking is also seeking us' for me is both a blessing and a spur on the journey.

And we are given help along the way. We can learn from Myths and stories of the great heroes and gods. Myths and fairy tales play a bit part in Jungian psychology for their metaphorical and symbolic content. At the very core of a fairy tale, just as at the core of a love affair, is a vision of wholeness. This is the central tenet of the power of these stories and resonates with us all. Most, if not all, fairy tales separate the masculine and feminine, which is unnatural and yet necessary if they are to find each other and be united. There is often a king without a queen, or a princess without a prince, and obstacles have to be overcome and challenges met in order for union to happen. The prince has to find his princess, the king his queen and so on. Their struggle to come together represents the struggle towards consciousness, and their union represents the outer union as well as the inner marriage we all seek. The prince needs to find his princess so that they become king and queen, and as such, reign over their happy kingdoms. The king and the queen represent conscious individuation and the fulfilment of the inner marriage. Princes and princesses are kings and queens in waiting – they are searching for their equal, the one who will recognise how special they are, how unique. Their union symbolises our potential sense of wholeness. The princess seeks someone who recognises her for who she truly is in her uniqueness. The prince seeks a princess worthy of him, who also recognises his majesty and his potential to become king.

Many of us travel down the wrong roads looking for love, especially if we are wounded and needy emotionally. Remaining open and, importantly, self-aware with a willingness to explore our own inner landscape and to mine our own mine or trek our own soul is always the answer. At times, however, we may need some respite from the alchemical cauldron and to take temporary refuge in a place of healing.

I find I am now tired and heavy with the burden of living life and trying to love unconditionally. Struggling to carry the weight of my emotional wounds when my heart hurts, it is time to head to the Rose Room. There I know I will receive healing and the much needed balm of unconditional love from the Divine Mother.

Chapter Six

The Rose Room

My heart belongs to you
I give myself to you to clear the pain,
The suffering, the sense of separation
That you experience in your everyday life
That's what I'm here for.
– Sai Maa

Before I met spiritual master and teacher Sai Maa, I knew her. I had a sense of her deep in my heart, tantalisingly elusive and yet always present. As the living embodiment of the Divine Feminine and the Mother Goddess, Sai Maa represents all that is sacred and divine in me as a woman. Through her beautiful body and luminous enlightened soul, she is a metaphor for my own Sacred Feminine nature. She radiates the soft, rose maternal healing energies of unconditional love. In my journey to heal my heart and my deeply feminine soul, she has been and still is pivotal. I am not a guru type person and was not at first inclined to follow the guidance of an old friend of mine who suggested I complete one of her healing journeys. "I know you are not a guru person but Sai Maa is different, she is a trained therapist and she works by combining therapeutic healing methods with spiritual energetic work – you will love it!" asserted my friend who had just returned fresh from one such experience. I was at that point going through a difficult time in my love relationship with my partner, and felt quite desperate for help and guidance. I decided to look Sai Maa up online. I was immediately struck and attracted by her. She was beautiful, and radiated as I said a pure rose healing luminous, feminine, graceful energy. I did not hesitate and signed up. It was a timely intervention and one that possibly changed my life.

Unconditional Love

Sai Maa is an ageless woman full of grace and always dressed beautifully in colourful Indian saris or Western clothes. She radiates feminine beauty and has all the energies of Aphrodite without any of the shadow. She is the epitome of unconditional love. Although small in stature she is majestic, splendid, strong and yet tender. If you are lucky enough to get physically close to her you will smell the intoxicating and exquisite scent of roses that emanates naturally from her skin. Most, especially the men, fall madly in love with her physical beauty; she holds a powerful attraction for everyone that meets her. As for myself, I wanted very much to be close to and held by her. I craved her enlightened Sacred Feminine wisdom and love. In the journey of profound healing, Maa spent several days with us engaging in intense inner work to uproot our core wounds, freeing us to begin creating a life unencumbered by the past. For Sai Maa, the roots of our wounds lie in our early life and most especially how we experienced being parented. During the course, when my work was completed (we each took turns on the 'carpet', choosing a mother and/or a father), I sat at her feet and asked her to place her hands on my head. I also asked if I could touch her, to which she acquiesced. I rested my head against her silk clad legs and felt her cradling me. I experienced such an intense feeling of love, I burst into tears. Maa was tender, and rubbing her arm to extract a pungent rose scent, she told me that going forwards, I would be able to sense her presence in my life through this scent. Indeed, I know Maa has come to me several times since, as several times I have been able to bask in her rose perfume. For me, her scent has become synonymous with unconditional love as has the rose. Today I only wear rose perfume and rose-infused cosmetics, hand and facial cleansing creams. My daily cleansing ritual with rose has become part of my healing journey and is my way of honouring my divine feminine self. And even though the heart chakra is traditionally seen as emanating a green colour, unconditional love for me is rose tinted. And the rose is a symbol for the Sacred Feminine.

And so we enter the Rose Room.

The Rose Room

It was a humid and sultry evening in East Florida when I entered Sai Maa's healing quarters, the top floor of a conference centre that had been specially adapted for the occasion. Personal healing sessions were an extra option available to us after the main conference events of the day. And one I had eagerly signed up for. Along with two other participants, I emerged from the lift and entered a beautiful, serene setting. The rooms were large and airy, mostly white walled with white gauze or voile coverings dividing certain parts of the room. Beautiful vases of flowers stood in every possible corner or on small tables dotted around, and dozens of soft candles lit up every corner of the rooms. It was dark except for the soft light from the multiple candles. An all-pervasive smell of roses filled the air and my senses – I felt I had entered a sacred healing temple. There was an anteroom to which you were led first as you prepared to enter the healing 'temple'. Everyone was dressed in white and each of us were assigned an assistant who helped us prepare for our personal healing session. Mostly there was silence although I cannot recall if there was a low background of spiritually uplifting music filling the rooms. I don't think so. What I remember most is, again, the most pervasive scent of rose and the feeling of unconditional love. The rooms were filled with healing energy and a sacred presence. We were handled very tenderly as we left our shoes, clothes and other 'worldly' possessions at the door and donned simple white garments. I felt very moved and close to tears most of the time. I had the sense of being held in the arms of the Divine Mother and knew that I was unconditionally loved and accepted.

After some time, the Divine Mother arrives – I know this from a subtle change in energy in the room and the faintest tinkle of bracelets and swish of silk. Sai Maa, in her embodiment of the Sacred Feminine, could be any of the goddesses, Mother Mary, Quan Yin, Isis or Mary Magdalene, she is all in the one, the Great Mother. With my heart full, I enter the Rose Room and am gently led to my healing table or plinth. It is dark except for the soft light of candles in the distance. I lie down and receive my healing. I enter a different dimension and am at peace.

When I awake or when I come to I am surprised to find I am alone with the Goddess. There are white and rose quartz crystals everywhere, and again, a delicate scent of roses fills the air. Dressed in elegant rose and white flowing garments, the Goddess invites me to come and sit with her on the white canopied seat that is her throne. She leans forwards and touches my heart and places a heart-shaped crystal on my chest and motions for me to sit at her feet. She places her hands on my shoulders and caresses then cradles my head. Bending down she tells me, "Write about this, write about the heart and the power of unconditional love to heal our sense of abandonment."

Then the Rose Room disappears and I am walking by the sea again. I begin to write.

Healing Abandonment

Only unconditional love can truly heal us and most especially heal our sense of abandonment. It can take a long time and many tears, meditations, hours in therapy and healing crystals to finally learn to heal our hearts. We may have to go on a long journey of discovery, not just to the bottom of the sea to uncover our deepest wounds hidden in the unconscious, but back to our early life experiences, including our births and being in our mother's womb. We may need to uncover how being in the womb was for us; what it was our mother experienced during her pregnancy with us, and most especially our birth experience. Of course, most of us do not have a conscious memory of our prenatal life or of our births. However, the memory is there nonetheless at a cellular body level, and can sometimes be accessed in therapy. Perhaps because of my own imprinting and experience I have often drawn clients who spontaneously are drawn back to their births when looking to heal their emotional wounds. Many feelings of abandonment, rejection and unworthiness stem from there. Behavioural patterns, underlying negative belief systems and difficulties in emotional relating and intimacy may have their origin in very early life and birth. What is certain is that our birth and prenatal life are formative soul experiences creating patterns we carry with us into later life.

This and more is the subject of my first book, *Songs from the Womb: Healing the Wounded Mother* (published in the USA as *Reclaiming the Spirituality of Birth*, Inner Traditions, 2000). There is a substantial body of work published in this area and the field of pre- and perinatal psychology is well established. Studies in both medicine and psychology and in the field of consciousness research confirm the findings, namely that our prenatal and birth experiences create imprints that are carried forward into later life. In *Songs from the Womb* I write: "Not so long ago, it used to be thought that the time in the womb did not count. It did not count because mental life began at birth. Unborn babies did not feel, think or dream and life in the womb was irrelevant in a way, as psychological life began at or soon after birth. However, recent studies tell us something quite different. They tell us not only that birth is a crucial, often traumatic experience for the baby, but also and equally importantly, that the prenatal experience is formative to future life. In other words, the quality and nature of a child's tenure in the womb influences not only how he or she will eventually experience birth, but also future life. It also tells us that the foetus and the unborn baby is not merely a developing biological organism, but a sophisticated evolving human being of immense sensitivity and capability."[13] More on this subject is readily available and is not the subject of this book. Suffice it to say here that healing a sense of abandonment will generally take you back to your very early life where you may have suffered some of your core wounds.

My work with my first therapist had indeed uncovered my own deep sense of abandonment originating in my very early life and at my birth. The 'empty ocean' in me, identified by my therapist, accounted for my deep sense of not being loved unconditionally, not being met, or not being accepted for who I truly was. It also explained the sense I had of being separated from everyone and utterly abandoned. I spent many weeks in an incubator growing and no doubt struggling for life. With my immature body and premature birth came many challenges, such as a difficulty breathing with ease and not being able to feed without the help of a nasogastric tube. I have a delicate and complex relationship to food and to nourishing myself to this day. My digestive system is highly sensitive and can tolerate only the purest of foods. And although I'm sure I received the best nursing and medical care possible at and after my birth, there was no emotional holding. Bonding, which is considered now the cornerstone of emotional development, was not something I experienced. I was separated from my mother who herself suffered from post-natal depression. And for many years and throughout my therapeutic journey I have at times felt a Perspex glass separates me from others. Common to many premature babies, I started my life in an incubator, so this is not surprising. The sense of disconnection, separation and aloneness was deeply rooted in the cells of my body, and when I would feel it, it would strike terror in my heart. This feeling could be triggered particularly in group therapeutic work such as workshops, and was totally involuntary. I write about my early journey in *Songs from the Womb,* and since our healing journey is always evolving, my early life may be less a source of suffering today, but it is still part of me. All that being said, by the time I entered the Rose Room and met Sai Maa many years later, I had healed some of my abandonment wound. Nonetheless, since emotional wounds are like roses and have many layers, the journey to healing my sense of abandonment is ongoing. I feel, however, that a very deep and perhaps fundamental core level was healed in me during the time with Sai Maa.

Mother Loss

A sense of abandonment or separation is common to many. As is a deep-seated feeling of not being loved unconditionally. My story is not unusual but it is unique to me, as your experience is to you. And you do not need to be born prematurely or to be separated from your mother in early life to feel abandoned. You may have had an absent, depressed or unavailable mother. Or you may have had a mother who was too busy, too preoccupied perhaps with other siblings or her own wounds, to pay attention to you or attune adequately to you. There are many variables. What is certain is that in order to heal your emotional wounds and restore your innate sense of wholeness, you may have to awaken to your sense of abandonment and learn to heal it. How do we do this? In one of my recent webinars, I address how we can heal this fundamental sense of abandonment. I listened back to it recently and was reminded that when seeking to heal the wound of abandonment, in essence what we are healing is a mother loss. Our mothers give us life, it is through our (biological) mothers that we come into this world and incarnate as human beings. Our mothers (and later our fathers and others) are responsible for how we experience a sense of being nurtured and loved. All souls need to be nurtured in order to develop into strong, emotionally secure human beings. As the late paediatrician and psychiatrist Donald Winnicott said, what we need is 'good enough' mothering. There are no ideals in this area, our parents are themselves human, and being so, subject to the same biological and psychic laws. They will have experienced their own 'brand' of mothering or nurturing which in turn will inform how they behave as parents. What we hope for indeed is a 'good enough' mother who has been able to give us, through tuning in to our 'unspoken' needs as babies and small children, a sense of what Winnicott called 'going on being'. A sense of being okay, a sense of trust and a feeling of being loved.

How do we heal a sense of abandonment? We have to learn to 'mother' ourselves and to love ourselves, a cliché I know, but this is nonetheless the only way. If, at our root and in our hearts, we have a sense of abandonment then attachment becomes difficult. There is a whole modality in psychology called Attachment Theory. Its creator John Bowlby noted that when the environment fails to meet the basic archetypal needs of the developing individual, psychological illness results. Bowlby "studied the psychological behaviour of very young children who were institutionalised, usually as a result of illness and noted that separation from their mothers had devastating consequences for their future development. The need to attach to a loving parent who is emotionally available on a consistent basis is a fundamental human need, present in every infant. Those infants and children in hospitals and orphanages for any length of time, suffer gravely, not merely due to separation from their mothers, but also from the unavailability of a consistent carer. Because of the nature of institutions, where different people are involved in the day to day care of the children, a child cannot attach itself to a mother surrogate. And secure attachment in early life helps us form healthy relationships later in life. Lack of this experience tends to make us anxious and insecure."[14] And whilst we may not have been raised in an orphanage or institution, we may also suffer from a 'failure to thrive' due to lack of consistent mothering or loving. It is a fact that attachment patterns are

The Soul & The Sea

formed in very early life and that these patterns are activated in later life and relationships. If we have not bonded well with our mothers or primary care givers, we may find it hard to form strong emotional attachments to others. Or we may find intimacy difficult, or be unable to be vulnerable and express our emotional needs and meet those of our lovers or partners. It is in love relationships that our childhood patterns are called up and our inner child is awakened. Our inner child can have many faces, the wounded child, the divine child or the orphan child to name a few. The orphan child is constellated in us through our sense of abandonment.

The Orphan Archetype: The Search for Belonging

It is our sense of abandonment that constellates our inner orphan. Healing our inner orphan is vital to re-establishing our sense of being whole, complete and pure in ourselves and to restore our trust in the universe. The orphan is propelled by a deep need to find home, a home being a place of belonging, or soul group. Indeed, the search to belong is so basic in us as to be archetypal. We may not be actual physical orphans in the 'real' world but many of us feel that we are psychological or emotional orphans. We may feel that we are not connected to our birth family or to the tribe or culture we have been born into. We feel different, as though we don't belong somehow. So, we have a longing, a longing deep within us to find home, to recover a sense of 'belonging'. It is clear that the need to 'belong' is so vital to our survival as members of the human race that we are universally compelled to search for it. Jungian author Clarissa Pinkola Estes writes:

Even though we have only heard or seen or dreamt a wondrous wild world that we belonged to once, even though we have not yet or only momentarily touched it, even though we do not identify ourselves as part of it, the memory of it is as a beacon that guides

104

us toward what we belong to.[15]

Estes refers to the story of the Ugly Duckling as metaphor for the universal search to belong. In this tale we have another fairy story that can help us by pointing the way. The story of the Ugly Duckling is all about healing a sense of abandonment through finding our true 'home', our flock – in essence our 'swan' nature. The essential energy of the orphan archetype is the search for belonging. Orphan children suffer a great deal, since they cannot find their true home. They feel abandoned and left to find their own way. Like all unmothered children, their instincts have not been sharpened and nurtured, so that they have to find their path, not through guidance but rather, like the Ugly Duckling, through trial and error. They have to find their way alone. You do not need to be actually orphaned to be an unmothered child, to be an ugly duckling. If you feel you were not nurtured in your essential self, if you feel not part of your birth family because you are 'different', the ugly duckling in you will push you to find your truth. Because of our innate drive to adapt and conform, our parents' attempt to mould us and make us what they want us to be will often develop in us a painful set of conflicting emotions. We want to be loved, but we feel rejected for who we truly are; we feel we cannot gain this love without compromising ourselves. Such a situation is very painful and wounding because, at base, our soul requires different things from us, and we find we cannot live our truth in our own family. The pain of not being true to ourselves may eventually drive us out of the nest, like the Ugly Duckling.

In my book *Love in a Time of Broken Heart* I wrote: "Being the outsider in a family constellates within us the orphan archetype. It is our Inner Orphan that impels us to find our true spiritual parents and family – a place where we can be ourselves, where our 'knowing' is accepted and acknowledged. The Orphan Child looks for his/her true home, where he/she will find nourishment and peace. Searching for and finding where we belong is a crucial and central part of individuation."[16] Individuation means coming to a sense of wholeness within. Many of us are outcasts, not fitting in with society and our families. We may find solace or a feeling of acceptance as we grow older and can gravitate towards like-minded people and groups. I have always felt I meet my true brothers and sisters at international psychological and spiritual conferences and events. Though we may all be speaking in different languages such as German, Dutch, Spanish or Italian as well as English, we all speak the same spiritual language of the heart. There is great comfort in finding your 'tribe' or spiritual soulmates. The theme of the exiled or outcast is archetypal and primeval, and forms part of a spiritual journey that is universal. The outcast is compelled to find his/her way back home. The trials of the orphan's journey serve a spiritual purpose. When the outcast or the orphan arrives home, he finds he has, like the Ugly Duckling, grown up.

The Ugly Duckling

The tale of the Ugly Duckling, as a metaphor for the orphan's journey, is a psychological and spiritual root story. Archetypal and universal, it is about our elemental search for belonging, a sense vital to the spiritual well-being of every individual. Without it we are bereft. Healing our inner orphan is recognising our journey from abandonment to a place of belonging as one of healing and spiritual growth. The Ugly Duckling's journey is also about persistence and endurance in the face of adversity. We can take lessons there; the Ugly Duckling's trials and hardship can help us in situations where we feel like giving up. His persistence and endurance pay off and show us that we should never give up on finding where we truly belong. And no matter how lost we are, we also have moments when a knowing comes in to warm us. This, I imagine, is what Jung refers to when he writes about finding the "helpful powers of our own nature" in our loneliness and abandonment. In profound vulnerability, a deeper intelligence comes through – from our own soul.

I have experienced this inner knowing that comes in, warming our emotional coldness when we feel lost. I can describe these as a felt sense of what felt right for me, such as being outdoors and following my 'true' nature. For me, following my nature has meant spending a lot of time alone, in nature itself, and most especially following the call of the sea. As a child I would rarely be found indoors, which always felt claustrophobic to me. I would play outside and spent many hours with our cats and dog and amongst animals generally. In later years when busy with my own children I would nonetheless try and find even twenty minutes to go out and sit on the rocks or by the sea, alone. There I would write in my journal and commune with my natural self. I would also read a lot. Perhaps this was my way of escaping into an exciting yet secure and safe world. The Ugly Duckling and the Orphan Child can help us develop the faith we need that we will eventually be united with our own kind, and that our abandonment will be healed. In psychological terms this amounts to coming to a sense of belonging to oneself. Individuating: feeling good in your own skin – a sense of spiritual home.

Healing our Inner Orphan

Healing our inner orphan is about consciously engaging with and navigating our journey to wholeness and enduring both the dark night and our abandonment. And surrendering to the process in the knowledge that our soul knows what it needs and is guiding us there. I am reminded of the words of the poet Rilke in *Letters to a Young Poet*:

So you must not be frightened, dear Mr. Kappus, if a sadness rises up before you larger than any you have ever seen; if a restiveness, like light and cloud-shadows, passes over your hands and over all you do. You must think that something is happening with you, that life has not forgotten you, that it holds you in its hand; it will not let you fall.[17]

The Ugly Duckling follows his nature and gets help along the way. One day, when his loneliness is at its peak, and he swims in a cold pond, he hears the cry of creatures that fly overhead, and his heart leaps. Their cries resonate somewhere deep inside him. He looks up and sees the most beautiful creatures he has ever seen, and they cry down at him. His heart rises and breaks at the same time, and he feels a desperate love for these great white birds that he cannot understand. After they leave, he is even more bereft. The swan's cry of recognition is painful, because it is the cry of belonging and the cry of loss at the same time. The Ugly Duckling had seen his kind and his soul family had recognised him. But he was not yet ready to join his family. He had not yet recognised the swan in him, and he still had growing to do. How often have we been in this painful situation; when a part of us feels abandoned and another is moving forwards towards home and a sense of place? How many of us, because of a painful childhood or life experience that has dented our sense of self, find it hard to recognise our inner swan, our divine natures? Divine nostalgia lies within us all at a deep core level. Hard to define and even harder to grasp, I feel it as a combined sense of grief and gratitude somewhere in the deepest recesses of my heart. I have come to recognise this energy as a tantalising glimpse of divine union, one that I long for.

Follow your nature and trust your soul to guide you. Healing abandonment means acknowledging yourself, and finding a safe place where you can be your true self. In essence, when we encounter unconditional love as I did in the Rose Room and with Sai Maa, and when we feel truly loved and accepted, we heal our sense of abandonment. Reminding us that early mothering and the sense of belonging activate in us innate wisdom, Pinkola Estes writes:

> We all have a longing that we feel for our own kind, our wild kind. Something great and big in us longs to be connected again with this primeval mother, and the ugly duckling in us will go on, until we find it.[18]

It is of course vital to journey in consciousness and remain open to receiving and working with our shadow. This involves being aware of the negative side of the orphan archetype which can keep us 'orphan' children all our lives by always projecting home onto others and repeating a pattern of finding 'surrogate' families to give us a sense of belonging instead of going within to find our home. We are all capable of recognising our 'inner swan' but often we need to 'grow into it'; to grow into a sense of our essential self to be able to reach a place in our hearts when we can love ourselves unconditionally. Patience, perseverance, endurance and resilience are the spiritual tools we need along the way. The poet Rilke expresses it well when he writes:

> Be patient toward all that is unsolved in your heart and try to love the questions themselves, like locked rooms and like books that are now written in a very foreign tongue. Do not now seek the answers, which cannot be given you because you would not be able to live them. And the point is, to live everything. Live the questions now. Perhaps you will then gradually, without noticing it, live along some distant day into the answer.[19]

Learning to Mother Yourself
Of fundamental importance to healing, however, is learning to mother yourself. I cannot overstate this. Most of us, have a tendency to look outside of ourselves for answers and for

healing and love. We look for 'surrogate' mothers and to our lovers and partners to give us the love we feel we didn't receive as children. If you feel unmothered or like the Ugly Duckling, alone, then it is essential you learn to love yourself. My first therapist used to tell me this all the time, and it is not something I welcomed at the time, since like most of us, I wanted to be mothered and loved (by someone else)! In my long years as a therapist I have myself repeated my analyst's words (probably to the aversion of some of my clients!), many times. When I was working and involved primarily with birthing and with helping women give birth, I grew used to being witness to the amazing embodiment of life in the physical body of a new mother. Birthing a new baby literally brings him or her into life. During pregnancy, however, the child's mother embodies him or her in an organic and natural way. So that when a client is suffering from a sense of not being adequately mothered or of having difficulty being on the planet, I tell them they must learn to "give birth to themselves". To embody themselves so that they are comfortable in their own skin with a deep sense of fundamental acceptance.

How can you learn to mother yourself? By listening to your inner voice, by answering the call from within. You can do this by journaling, by writing your dreams so that you are indeed weaving, giving birth to your soul and the images from your psyche. By doing what you love or what makes your heart sing. In my own life this has been a gradual evolution. I have had to learn to not only fill the lacuna, the empty ocean, but to fill it with love and with gratitude and acceptance for my beautiful soul and my tender body. My mother the sea helps me as do the earth and land creatures, and the spirit of nature and life itself. Mystical and wise women along the way have helped weave me into existence as have many of my soulmates both men and women and wonderful and gifted healers that shared my path. They continue to do so. Being in nature and also spending tender time with myself in my daily body ritual of cleansing and nourishing is part of mothering myself. I have massages as much as I can and long baths by candlelight with fragrant oils. My bathroom is dotted with shells and corals I have collected from the sea and shores all over the world. I like to be surrounded by stones I pick from the shore. I imagine I am connecting and communing with my Divine Feminine and Mother through such items. I pick the feathers left by transient storm birds and seagulls and place them near my writing desk. I imagine that by doing this, I am communing with the great Spirit of Life.

Mother yourself by spending time alone or with those you love, removing yourself as much as you can from situations that are causing you stress or that are causing you to shut down. Most of all, mother yourself by accepting yourself as you are, and crucially, avoid self-criticism. Know that you are perfect and complete as you are and that you are loved and held by the Divine Mother. And when you lose faith or fall down, as we all do from time to time, remember the following. Many of you will know the poem "Footprints in the Sand", of the man who dreams he walks on the beach with the Lord and looking back over his life he sees that in the most troubled and saddest times there were only one set of footprints. When he passes over, he asks why God had abandoned him in his hour of need. The Lord answered: "My precious child, I love you and will never leave you never, ever, during your trials and testings. When you saw only one set of footprints, It was then that I carried you." Anchor yourself in this knowing. As I have from my time in the Rose Room.

The Goddess appears again and suggests we take a walk outside in the verdant and luscious land. There is more she wants me to see and discover deep into the forest. We must go on a journey together until we come to the Green Room, hidden deep in the forest.

Chapter Seven

The Green Room

The Goddess and I walk a long time. We traverse different lands and terrains, sometimes crossing bridges and entering green lush meadows before ascending steep mountains and descending again onto wild rocky plains. I lose all sense of time, but I am aware that day changes into night and night into day. And at times it feels as though we are flying. We are going a long way; I feel safe in her guidance and love. We are accompanied by a warm breeze and a sense of purpose; I feel no tiredness and have no desire to rest. At last, we arrive at the edge of a large lusciously green forest and sit a while on a grass-covered low bank. By this time we are accompanied by melodious birds chirping us to our destination and I'm aware of a myriad of other tiny unseen creatures playing and scampering around us. I look down and see we are both now clothed in green gowns and our feet are bare. The Goddess stands and indicates we are to go into the forest. She walks now with a sense of purpose and I follow, glad of her guidance through the narrowing paths that lead to the centre, the thickest part of the forest. I am aware of music, a low whistling that seems to come from the tall tree and grasses swaying in the light breeze. It is getting dark. Ahead of me I see a clearing and several cave-like entrances that appear above the ground. Each entrance is partially covered by undergrowth and long grasses. The Goddess enters the largest opening and I follow; the grasses part as we enter. I am inside a large, cavernous opening, it is dark and humid. There is no light except from small candles flickering here and there casting a brownish dim glow on the cave walls. A strong earthy smell fills my nostrils; I feel safe and nurtured. The entrance to the Green Room is through here. I know this somehow, and as I look around I notice that I am now alone. I am not frightened, and sit on the ground. I am waiting to be seen, I know a presence will be here soon to guide me. I wait, serene and peaceful. Very soon, the Goddess appears again and takes me by the hand. We are now entering one of the other caves; we seem to be deep inside the earth somehow and I see there are many women of different ages involved in different undertakings. I have a panoramic bird's eye view. Each cave leads to the next and in each respective cave lives a goddess or wise woman. One is busy planting and harvesting herbs, and making potions and remedies. Another is sweeping the hearth and busy guarding her home and minding her children. In another, the wise woman is surrounded by animals to whom she is tending. One is washing her hair in a beautiful crystal blue lake, surrounded by her maidens. Another is singing and playing the lyre. And in one, the last one, a wise woman, majestically dressed in green, sits at a table by candlelight, writing. She welcomes me and asks me to sit. This is the Green Room. There is a sense of beauty and creativity, fertile life and new birth here. The earth goddess hands me the pen and says, *"Write about creativity; write about renewal and new life, write about how deep is our soul."*

I take up the pen and begin.

Soon the Green Room disappears.

Nature & the Soul

You could never arrive at the limits of the Soul, no matter how many roads you travelled, so deep is its mystery.
– Heraclitus

The Wild Atlantic Way
Connecting with the energy of Mother Nature puts one in instant rapport with the cycles of life – birth, death and rebirth.

Such a connection helps us awaken to our own wild nature and a sense of belonging to all that is alive. It is well recognised that the natural world and being in nature has a calming and healing effect on people. I have always keenly felt the healing power and sacred nature of the earth and the sea. You cannot be born and raised in a remote rural coastland and not be somehow connected to the elements. Our home bordered on the sea in the farthest most westerly corner of Ireland. A bleak, barren and desolate landscape that could be harsh as it could be beautiful, the Wild Atlantic Way reveals to those that travel her paths something mysterious, deep and wild that calls to our molten hearts and the depths of our soul. All along the West coast of Ireland has been designated the Wild Atlantic Way, and they say that the sights and sounds of the Way will reinvigorate your soul and tease your senses. It's wild, it's untamed, it's rugged and full of the mystery of life, like the mists that descend and disappear without warning. Those who live here on the edge grow used to being remoulded, and at times wonder how it happened without our even noticing. Being born here, I have always been deeply connected to the land, to the earth, and I know I am rooted here with roots that go deep. And although in my adult life I have migrated and lived in different countries and cities too, I always hankered after the land of my birth. Something elemental in the waves of the sea, the cries of the gulls and the whispering of the wind connects me with all creation and with my soul. My feminine soul with tendrils inextricably entwined with the goddess and mother earth. I draw essential nourishment from her as she continues to inspire me.

Everything is wild, here on the Wild Atlantic Way; the sea is at its roughest, the wind its loudest and the land harsh and unforgiving and yet incredibly beautiful. If you walk the Wild Atlantic Way you will go North or South and always remain in the West. The same West that my father came to over half a century ago, with very little other than his family and a desire for freedom. Standing on the beach in front of our home on the farthest western point he could find on this rugged land, he would stare out to sea and tell us we were as far away as possible from de Gaulle, France's then president, of whom he was not a fan. Next stop America. America, I marvelled, a new land somewhere out there beyond, that people called the new world. And it seemed to my childish eyes that we lived on a kind of ledge jutting out to sea – an Island of its own and that this meant freedom. On clear days I would stand on the same spot scrunching up my eyes and imagine I could see the faintest glimmer of land – America. A land of hope and new life. Nonetheless, life here on this rugged ledge of the Wild Atlantic was what you made it, and it seemed to me somehow, that living here gave you wings. On wild blustery nights, we lay cuddled up in bed listening to the howling wind and wondered if the roof would cave in. On particularly wild nights, fearing take-off, I would secretly secure myself to my bed with an old belt of my father's in case Mary Murray's banshee would come for me. Mary, an equally wild village woman whose only sin was to be born with one maimed hand, was my mother's maid and my nanny. Electricity would come and go and wasn't something you could count on, but this didn't bother me for I loved the candles and paraffin lamps my father would puff up to keep us warm. On those days we were kept in the kitchen, and huddled close to the range, reading late into the day and sometimes falling asleep by the fire.

I have often wondered where my deep-rooted need for freedom came from. And although being a free spirit whilst simultaneously having deep roots may sound paradoxical, I am comforted by the words of Greek philosopher Heraclitus, *"You could never arrive at the limits of the Soul, no matter how many roads you travelled so deep is its mystery."* Whether it was something in the land or my upbringing that constellated in me this free spirit, what is certain is that my soul chose to incarnate here, perhaps many times. It was nonetheless many years and many experiences later that I discovered or realised that my soul connects with the land energies, the fairies and the goddesses in my sleep state and that I had the power to shape shift. Born psychic intuitive, I felt deeply for the animals and the earth around me and always felt more whole and true to my 'real' self when I was outdoors. Our proximity to the Atlantic ensured I was totally immersed in nature, with the sound of the waves often lulling me to sleep. The sea called me often and awakened in me my own Sacred Feminine and sense of being part of a divine whole. As my spiritual studies and experiences increased I came to know the vastness of our soul and the essential nature of consciousness; we are part of the great divine force. We were born in God's image and we carry that power within us. Also, we have a soul contract and a destiny. We are here for a reason, the reason being to serve God or the divine within. We may not be conscious of our soul contract and it may take some time to awaken to our divine purpose. Our wise soul knows this which is why most of what we do is in service to our soul. Our relationships for example, whether we have experienced them as good or bad, hurtful or nourishing, are all part of our soul's learning. We all have our own unique path to tread, our own soul destiny. Some of us will feel God or the Divine through music or writing, others through art or drama, some through giving birth to and nurturing children, some through their relationships, many through living in nature, and others through their work. When you are truly tapping into your creativity, to the life force in you, you are experiencing your divinity with the ability to 'flow' with life. The sticking point, however, the fly in the ointment, is the ego. Most of us have some growing up to do before we can fully awaken to our divine purpose. Part of the journey to spiritual awakening involves learning to handle and relativize our ego.

The Ego & the Self

My training in depth psychology has been particularly useful when it comes to understanding the difference between the ego and the (true) self. For Jung, the ego is merely the driver of the personality, whereas the Self (with a big S) is in essence the archetype of totality, of wholeness. It is the Self that guides us through the process of Individuation – of coming into wholeness. The Self can be described as the regulating centre of the psyche; a transpersonal power that transcends the ego. The Self's inherent purpose is the attainment of the fullest possible self-realisation in the psyche and in the world. In encompassing our dreams and aspirations, the Self has access to a much wider realm of experience than the Ego, which is privy purely to our conscious preoccupations. The archetype of the Self provides the means of adaptation not only to the environment but also to God and the life of the spirit. It encompasses not just the personality but also our aspirations, what we can be or become along with our spiritual yearnings. Jung differentiated Self from Ego as follows:

> The ego stands to the self as the moved to the mover, or as object to subject, because the determining factors which radiate out from the self – surround the ego on all sides and are therefore subordinate to it. The self, like the unconscious, is an a priori existent out of which the ego evolves.[20]

And so we can see that, in essence, we need to transcend the drives and desires of the ego to progress spiritually and to become more conscious. Thriving on separation, Ego desires are typically externally driven which is not the case with the Self. Becoming more psychologically self-aware is also essential to heal our emotional wounds, and indeed, access our creativity. Our soul may want more from us than the narrow life our ego is comfortable with so that if we want to truly evolve we have to learn to 'let go'. Letting go of our old identities, our attachments to certain goals or outcomes, even relationships we may have 'outgrown', is never easy. It is never easy because our ego likes to be in control and letting go is not something the ego wants to do. Indeed, as I learnt from Sai Maa, the ego's very 'raison d'être' or job, is to separate us from our higher selves. I see the Self as the psychological version of the higher self, meaning, the whole of us, incorporating our spiritual aspirations and our soul's purpose. And true creativity comes directly from our soul, bypassing the ego.

Complexes

Nonetheless, formation of the ego is a necessary part of personality development. All humans need a certain amount of 'ego' to be able to function in the world. Indeed, from a psychological perspective, an inadequately formed ego can be problematic. People with weak egos may suffer a great deal and find the world a difficult place to inhabit. Developing in early life, our egos mature generally by young adulthood and become the drivers of our personality. It is commonly only at middle age that we begin to look to our greater selves. We seek what we could become, our spiritual aspirations and the call of our souls perhaps to live a 'greater' life. The first part of life is busy with growing up, leaving our parents, creating our own homes, careers, families and so on. At some stage, generally approaching middle age, we begin to ask ourselves, "Is this all there is?" or "Why am I here?" and put a call out to our souls to find greater meaning and purpose to our lives. This call can come in different forms; it may be an illness or health issue, the ending of a major relationship or a form of 'mid-life crisis' forcing us to change our way of being.

When we begin this soulful journey we will often be employed in uncovering and resolving our 'complexes'. A complex is an autonomous set of impulses grouped around certain kinds of energy-charged ideas and emotions. We all have complexes. What impressed Jung most about the complex is its autonomy. Complexes behave like independent beings, wrote Jung. When in the grip of a complex we have a feeling of being carried by a great force of energy or inflation. Inflation can be described as a feeling of power in which we are blown up by an unknown force that is not our own. That being said, we usually encounter our complexes through projection. Projection is the visualisation of a complex (usually in another person) and it is the emotional colouring that will tell us whether or not we are caught in a projection. We can observe this in any argument when our emotions become triggered, when we get 'hot under the collar' or tearful in situations that wouldn't normally warrant such emotion. Complexes are not only negative but can have a positive attraction such as 'falling in love'. It is often considered that we fall in love with an aspect of our soul, as yet unknown, that we see in the love object. The thing that attracts us is a projection of latent negative or positive traits as yet undeveloped. This means, for example, that we can be attracted by something which 'wants to be known'.

We can be called by our complexes as we journey towards spiritual growth. Complexes become constructive when made conscious and integrated. If/when this happens it means resolution or integration is necessary before we can let go and move on. In my own life and those of my clients, I have found that the complex will keep showing up, maybe in different guises, until we learn the lesson. There is always a soul lesson hidden in our complexes. When we have overcome the challenges inherent to the complex, we grow and move up a notch in our spiritual evolution. I remember consulting a wise woman and spiritual teacher some years ago who told me that I was like someone who had been told they could walk on water but was still holding on to the boat! I was still caught up in my abandonment complex which meant it was hard for me to fully trust. Even though I had progressed on my spiritual path, fear and lack of trust was holding me back from wholly inhabiting myself. Uncovering and integrating our complexes is a necessary part of our journey to spiritual growth and awakening.

Trekking your Soul

To learn to uncover and integrate your complexes and what might be holding you back from living a full, authentic and soulful life you will need to go within and trek your soul. Unfettered access to your creativity depends on you being available to yourself and not called away by your ego concerns. One such way is for you to be present to your inner life and the life that wants to come through you. As I've heard several spiritual teachers say, sometimes we have to get out of our own way! We may have a strong (ego) idea of what we want or 'need', such as a new car, bigger house, better job or relationship, when in fact if we pay attention to our subtle inner voice, our soul may want something quite different from and for us. Our true creativity may be waiting in the wings. It may show up in our dreams for example. Dreams, as the voice of our soul, speak to us through images and symbols.

On my own therapeutic journey I have had numerous, vivid dreams which I always recorded in my dream journal and took to my analyst. Some of these dream images held a numinous, transformative energy which I was able to harness in service to my soul growth. In my dream/visualisation deep into the forest above, I was given a glimpse of the Sacred Feminine at work, the Great Mother whose fierce love nourishes and keeps me safe. The experience of witnessing the earth goddesses in such a way had a profound effect on me. I remember vividly in the early years of being in psychotherapy, that I shared this dream with my analyst. When I described the different wise women/goddesses busy in their respective caves deep in the earth, I remember she was very moved. The vibrancy, energy, and sacredness of the creative Great Mother was palpable in the room as I spoke. There was nothing my therapist could or needed to say. We both felt it and knew a sacred numinous event had taken place. My inner work and soul evolution took a growth spurt after this dream. The imagery has stayed with me and propelled me into more writing and teaching, rooting an ancient knowing in my bones so that I came to trust that I am indeed being held in the arms of the Divine and of Mother Nature.

Making Tracks: Connecting with the Father Energy

The facility with which we can access our creativity also depends on other factors, such as how we experienced our early life. Our parents have a role here, and more specifically our fathers. This is the subject of my second book, *Reclaiming Father: The Search for Wholeness in Men, Women and Children*. How we were fathered or how we experienced our fathers has a direct impact on our creativity, and most particularly, on our ability to follow through and bring our creativity out into the world. The Sacred Masculine is the counterpart of the Sacred Feminine and it is he that guides us into the world. In the words of Jungian author and analyst Robert Bly:

> *The father gives with his sperm a black overcoat around the soul, invisible in our black nights. He gives a sheathing or envelope or coating around the soul made entirely of intensity, shrewdness, desire to penetrate, liveliness, impulse, daring.*[21]

In *Reclaiming Father* I write about the formative impact of the father to the psychological development of his child.[22] Fathers have a different energy to mothers and their influence on the developing psyches of their children is distinct. It is a father, for example, who helps the child separate emotionally from his mother, a seminally important task, especially for boys. Whereas mother's role is archetypally to give birth to and nurture her children, father's is to protect and guide the child out into the world. In *Reclaiming Father* I write how the analogy of a bird's nest can be used to describe the father's protective function.[23] The nest has a double container, one inside the other. The outer layer is rough because it secures the nest to the tree – it is on the outside. The inner layer of the nest is soft and maternal. Father's energy is more about boundaries and protection and can help the child activate his own creativity. Father gives the child structure and helps him or her strive towards goals and establish a sense of identity separate from mother. Father is very important in helping the child negotiate and make tracks in the world. *Reclaiming Father* also addresses the negative impact that absent fathers in particular have on their sons, but also their daughters.

It seems that although we may be creative, it is the quality and nature of our internalised father energy that will determine how well we can ACTIVATE our creativity. Giving form or giving birth to our ideas and bringing them out into the world necessitates a strong animus. Just as the anima for men represents their feminine counterpart, the animus archetype in a woman is our masculine energy; he generally has the face of our fathers, the first man in our lives.

I learnt from my own father to follow my dreams, my aspirations. Not afraid to step outside the norm, my father through his political beliefs ended up leaving his home in France and becoming an exile in another land – Ireland. From being a civil servant in a city he became a fisherman by running a shellfish business in the West of Ireland. He had to begin again and had no fear of making a new start. And although my father was a gentle kind of spirit he must have had a backbone of steel to be able to navigate the choppy waters of post-war exile and build for us a home in a foreign land. Not to mention learn a new language. Both of my parents grew to love our new home in Ireland, the wild land and the people. Although I count myself as a creative person, I have sometimes been held back by a lack of trust, which has meant that at the eleventh hour, I grow frightened that I cannot 'finish' the task on hand. On the other hand, my partner and many others have told me they consider me fearless. Indeed, I am somebody who has travelled all over the world, often alone, and am undaunted by new beginnings. I can truly say I have a courageous spirit as my father must have had, when approaching middle age, he landed in Ireland with nothing but his wit and his young family. A landing and exile I have long been grateful for, since it has given me my soul journey here in my soul home by the sea. And perhaps too my father's actions, some decades ago now, have given me the wings to fly and the roots to come back to. A potent metaphor for the sacred marriage of the Divine Masculine and Divine Feminine.

But there are other archetypes we must negotiate before we can fly and be truly grounded in our selves.

Inner Archetypes: Victim, Prostitute, Child and Saboteur

There can be many reasons why we may have difficulty accessing our creativity and being in the 'flow' of life. Fear is one major reason. Sometimes we can be fearful without realising it and settle for a complacent life free of challenges. Or we might seek refuge and escape in a safe zone of our own creation, retreating from life. Our ego desires, our belief systems, issues from our childhood, being employed by our complexes can all act as blocks to living a soulful and passionate life. During my Healing From Within workshops I would take participants on a healing journey to uncover and release emotional wounds that were holding them back from living fulfilling and happy lives. In the course of this soul work, we would identify the four main survival archetypes that live with us in our everyday lives.

First identified by Caroline Myss, these are the inner Victim, Child, Prostitute and Saboteur. The Child archetype embodies innocence and purity. Our creativity is intimately bound up in the child archetype so, for example, if we have had an emotionally stark childhood we may find it hard to express our creativity in a healthy way. Children naturally learn through play and if there is serious impingement on their sense of security, of being loved, or of 'going on being', then accessing their own creativity will be difficult. Reactive behaviour (such as people pleasing, over or under compliance) will replace being true to themselves and many children will develop 'false' selves in order to fit in. Reactive behaviour is normal; we all have to adapt to the environment and conditions in which we grow. However, these behavioural patterns, formed in childhood, often continue well into adulthood when they are no longer needed, hampering our ability to be our true creative, divine selves.

To be able to bring your creativity to life you need to have healthy self-esteem. The feeling and experience of being accepted for who we are is fundamental to developing our self-esteem. The Victim archetype relates directly to self-esteem and personal power. The core issue for victims is whether it is worth giving up their sense of empowerment to avoid taking responsibility for their independence. Many people with a strong 'victim' archetype find it hard to take responsibility for their lives and prefer to remain 'victims' of their past/childhood. Such an attitude is really an affliction and prevents any growth or creativity since the victim remains in a prison of his own making. An example is a person who might identify themselves solely as a 'survivor', ignoring their greater part – a soulful human being made of starlight.

The Saboteur archetype relates to how we manage choice and change in our lives. The core issue for the Saboteur is fear of change. When there is such a fear, one might become obsessive compulsive in adherence to strict routines, for example, and shy away from embracing change or anything new into our lives. Again fear is a motivational factor in such behaviour. This archetype makes its energy felt through disruption, so that we sabotage our opportunities for advancement and relationships that might be good for us. It is the saboteur in us that destroys our creative attempts and our chances to become more conscious and evolve spiritually.

The Prostitute archetype then embodies faith and trust in the universe and ourselves. When we don't have enough faith or self-belief for example, we will generally 'prostitute' ourselves in return for emotional, material, or physical security. Many of us can indeed relate to this, especially if we have had difficult childhoods or an emotionally insecure early life. We might 'prostitute' ourselves by attaching ourselves to inappropriate 'surrogate' mothers or fathers to provide what we feel we lacked in childhood. But it will be at a cost and usually not without compromising ourselves. Of course we have elements of all these archetypal energies within us which, one way or the other, we will be playing out in our lives. As said, they are our survival archetypes.

In my own life I can certainly relate to the archetype of the Prostitute. Not feeling basically secure, loved or accepted for who I was, I 'prostituted' myself several times by, for example, staying in unhealthy relationships too long. Fearful of being alone or not managing alone, I lacked trust in both myself and the universe to look after me. Thinking about it, I feel it is significant that I really only accessed my true creativity in middle age! My first book was written in my early forties. My emotional background and the deprivation I felt in my early life formed an overlay that obscured my soul path and my innate gifts. At a subtle level, I felt unable to be totally myself and probably compromised myself in several ways in the service of my deep-seated fear of abandonment. During my therapeutic soul journey, I gradually realised that, in essence,

I am a Warrior and a Pioneer with a mission to accomplish. It was some time, however, before I could inhabit my Warrior self. It took a while for me to get used to the sense of aloneness that accompanies the Warrior, who always walks alone. Being by nature a maverick and a pioneer is again not something easy to inhabit. It means leaving the pack, something Jung insists is an integral part of individuation. Daring to be different, stepping out of the security blanket of the 'norms' dictated by family and society, takes courage and can be a lonely path. I did discover, however, by living some long days into it, the difference between loneliness and solitude. And I have lived a lot of my adult life alone as well as enjoying partnership and family life, so that I can truly say, I feel alone and yet never more connected to all.

Healing From Within

By now you will have understood that I work from both a depth psychological and spiritual perspective. And although my training and experience in psychology can be seen as a hindrance when looked at from purely spiritual eyes, I believe that it is important to blend both when we are looking to grow spiritually and to heal. As I wrote in *Love in a Time of Broken Heart* more than a decade ago now, "I am aware that in the main, those in the psychotherapeutic camp sometimes lack the trust necessary to believe in the power of the transcendent or the divine in our lives, and those in the 'spiritual' or healing camp can be ignorant or dismissive of the importance of the psychological dimension. Spiritual teachers and alternative healers sometimes dismiss the suffering or the graft work necessary for true change and the necessity of embracing the shadow or wounded aspects of our lives. Psychologists, on the other hand, with a tendency to concretising human life, can be in danger of remaining stuck in emotional wounds of early life." A middle ground is necessary if we are to heal from within – the only way to heal. In the years since, I have seen this middle ground evolve organically as more and more people are awakening to their own divinity and ability to heal. Relying less on medics or experts and 'people out there' to offer a panacea for their healing, people are willing to look within to find their own remedies to heal their soul pain. And so putting on my psychological hat, delving into our psyches, trekking our soul and uncovering the patterns that no longer serve us are integral parts of healing and spiritual growth. To this I would add that the only reason to 'go back' is to 'go forward'! Meaning, it is important not to dwell in the past but merely to 'pass by' – become aware of, integrate, and move on.

Workbook and Exercises

Patterns emerge out of the deepest layers of the unconscious and are generally inherited, forming part of our ancestral and family lineage and experience. From a depth psychological perspective, you will need to think about what patterns you have inherited from your mother and from your father. Spend some time with each parent, writing down what you feel you have inherited from both. For your mother, write down what her qualities and what her patterns were/are. Then do the same with your father. For mother you might for example include nurturing, or coldness, gentleness or harshness and so on. For father you might include courage, ruthlessness, fear or whatever. Spend some time with each, making sure you write down both negative and positive traits. It is not a fact that we only associate nurturing qualities with our mothers and authoritative ones with our fathers. I have many times worked with clients whose primary source of love and nurturing came from their father. You might have inherited and internalised a sense of love and consistency from your father, and an energy of unreliability and coldness from your mother. It doesn't matter what you have internalised or inherited from each, what matters is uncovering the patterns within you that are still playing out in your life and which no longer serve you. This might be a tendency to compliancy or people pleasing for example. Or a desire to control your relationships. Whatever your patterns, once you have brought them to consciousness, it is much easier to let them go, especially when you can see they no longer serve your soul.

In terms of accessing your inner feminine and masculine, the polarities within you, you will need to look at how you internalised and related to both parents individually. To get a sense of your Inner Feminine you will need to look at your mother and your relationship with her. Ask yourself such questions as: How did I perceive my mother? How did I experience her? What relationship did I have with her? What did she teach me about being a woman? Or, for men, what did she teach me about the feminine? How might your early relationship with her be operating in your relationships right now? Then look at your father and your relationship with him to find the energy of your Inner Masculine. Repeat the same questions and exercise for your father.

Changing our Patterns

To live in this world, you must be able to do three things: to love what is mortal; to hold it against your bones knowing your own life depends on it; and, when the time comes to let it go, to let it go.
– Mary Oliver

To change patterns and belief systems that no longer serve us, we must go within and invoke the Sacred Feminine. Psychological understanding can indeed uncover our patterns but it can be more difficult to learn how to let go and change outworn patterns, replacing them with new healthier qualities. In the course of my work with Sai Maa, I attended several workshops dedicated to releasing our patterns. Entitled the Patterns

Journey, we were led to become aware of and release deeply rooted patterns from our childhoods that no longer served our spiritual growth. We began first with awareness (1). Once we had identified and become aware of a pattern, the next step in the process was acceptance (2). Acceptance is more profound than it sounds. Most of us have great difficulty with acceptance, being in the now and taking things as they are. This is usually because our self-acceptance is something we have to work hard at. Our inner critic is always ready to pounce! This again is something my analyst used to remind me of, telling me I was actually very self-critical. Spiritually, I have learnt that what we generally perceive as negative emotions such as jealousy, envy, anger, fear and so on are classed as of lower frequency. Indeed, since in essence, there is only love, and fear is the opposite to love, these lower frequency emotions all stem from fear. Fear of losing, fear of being judged, fear of being abandoned and so on. When we are in the grip of fear we contract or close down our heart energy, whereas love expands us. Step three of the process is very important. Step three involves taking this lower frequency energy and lifting it into our heart (3). There is now an empty space in our psyche as it were, where the old pattern resided; we need to replace it with a new Divine quality (4). So fear will be replaced by its opposite, love and trust. The clarity of the pattern will release the clarity of the Divine quality, through self-confidence, knowingness, forgiveness and love. The process of letting go of an outworn pattern and then replacing it with a higher frequency Divine pattern is profound. The change in energy will be noticeable and beneficial, just as the energy that is released when you confide in someone or cry for example.

Step five involves affirmations and mindful conscious practice to anchor the new higher frequency divine pattern into our physical being (5). Explaining that constant and repetitive thought forms create neural pathways (if you say, "I am abandoned" or "I feel abandoned" often enough it forms a neural pathway), Sai Maa impressed on us the need to feed the new pattern, like watering a seed daily. This can be done through daily affirmations and meditation. For 'fear' substitute 'trust' for example. To change a lower frequency pattern to a higher frequency one based on love and trust, it must be repetitive so that it creates a new neural pathway. Reminding us that our patterns, like our complexes, grab us every now and then, Maa impressed on us the need for discipline. Daily meditations and affirmations, like repetitive mantras, serve to anchor a new knowing, a new higher frequency energy into our bodies and consciousness. Repetitive affirmation and the use of "I AM" (followed by the quality, such as Trust – "I am Trust") sixteen times is very powerful. Affirmation and commitment to action is necessary. I end my relationship with control and send it back to its source; I give back and take in the opposite. "I end my relationship with abandonment and send it back to its source."

After one such workshop with Sai Maa, I remember I came home with renewed energy and determination to finally rid myself of the pattern of fear of abandonment that was still cropping up in my life. I was no stranger to this work and to the power of affirmations, but found it hard to commit to the daily discipline of watering my new seed, that of trust, in this instance. I had gone to the patterns workshop with my heart, once again, in tatters. A lost lover and life partner had returned briefly into my life and I had had hopes of a reconciliation and of a life spent together at last. However, despite bending backwards to accommodate him, my ex-partner had once again betrayed me by never returning from the short trip he had made to his family in the Southern hemisphere. So, understandably, trust was not high on my spiritual agenda at this time and my heart was hurting. Nonetheless, my determination, bolstered by renewed energy, eventually produced results. Practising the letting go process and daily affirmations and meditation didn't stop my heart pain but lessened it considerably. Most importantly, I did feel a shift in energy, I felt lighter and more grounded in myself and my ability to trust. I am sure that I took a leap in letting go of my old abandonment pattern.

Committing to something for forty days, according to Sai Maa, is very powerful. Since the brain is malleable, the new higher frequency gradually dissolves the lower frequency energy. Sai Maa's mantra had been: "Create your life today for the future you want." Take action for what you want to see in your life. The affirmation, "I construct a new life with new energy," was anchored in me.

I have been writing a long time. It is almost dark and I lay down my pen. I leave the Green Room and make my way out of the earth caves and into the forest. I feel energised by my time in the life-giving earth and meeting with the Goddesses. I know what I must do. But first, I need to pay a visit to the Purple Room. There I will reconnect with my soul in a very particular way.

Chapter Eight

The Purple Room

You have no need to travel anywhere
Journey within yourself
Enter a mine of rubies and bathe
In the splendour of your own light.
– Rumi

Many years ago, I was told that I have a mauve, deep blue and purple coloured aura. At that time, I was quite new to clairvoyance although always attracted to all aspects of energy medicine, mediumship and the spiritual in general. As a natural clairsentient, I felt or intuited rather than 'saw', and was in awe of clairvoyance. I didn't think much more about my aura colours then, being more concerned with strengthening my boundaries so that the 'hole' that had been noted by a senior member of the College of Psychic Studies years earlier could be closed. However, sometime later I attended and presented at a psychology and spirituality conference in New Mexico, USA, where I was fortunate to meet Donna Eden, pioneer in energy medicine. Queueing to ask her to sign her book *Energy Medicine* which I had just purchased, I was delighted to share a few words with her as she signed it. I remember she looked at me smiling broadly as she asked my name before writing on the cover page in large flowing purple writing. When I got back to my seat I opened the book and read, *"Dear Benig, you have lovely lavender and rose energies and a real healing force, love Donna Eden"*. Needless to say I was delighted. But what struck me was that here again, a clairvoyant had confirmed my predominant aura 'colours'.

I have always loved and been drawn to mauve, lavender,

rose and violet. Although I hadn't formally 'studied' energy medicine, I instinctively 'knew' about chakras and auras from a very young age. At various times in my life, my inner knowing has been triggered, generally through important developmental and biological milestones, such as pregnancy and childbirth, for example. Drawn to various healing modalities, when I needed help, I opted for alternative or natural medicine as opposed to allopathic when at all possible. I choose to give birth naturally, at home, to avoid the medical management of childbirth which I instinctively knew went against nature often causing trauma and soul loss to women and their babies. As I wrote in *Songs from the Womb*, the benefits of technology in medicine are undoubted, but they need to be balanced with respect for the human soul and the innate intelligence of nature and natural processes. Childbirth is a natural process. I have met many physicians and medical professionals who understand this, including doctors who incorporate energy medicine into their practice. At a world conference about twenty years ago I was particularly fortunate to meet with and discuss the limitations of using forceps in childbirth and the healing tools of a young Russian doctor specialised in healing birth trauma. The crown chakra is often damaged during an instrumental delivery, he contended. Thankfully, with the existence of cranial sacral therapists and others, such damage can be undone and healed, both on a physical and emotional level.

Purple or violet is the colour of the crown chakra and is associated with imagination and spirituality as well as royalty. Purple or violet colours assist those who seek the meaning of life and spiritual fulfilment; these colours are known to expand our awareness, connecting us to a higher consciousness. For this reason it is associated with transformation of the soul, and both spiritual seekers and philosophers are often attracted to it. I further read that the colours purple and violet represent the future, the imagination and dreams, while spiritually calming the emotions. They inspire and enhance psychic ability and spiritual enlightenment, while, at the same time, keeping us grounded. It is no surprise that I was drawn to the psychology of Carl Jung who considered dreams to be the royal road to the unconscious. Dreamwork has been a big part of my therapeutic journey, and I continue to write and work with my dreams to this day. As a doorway to our unconscious and to the vast collective field of energy and consciousness available to all of us, dreams are the voice of our soul. She may not speak to us in our everyday spoken language; she speaks in images and symbols, whispering into the ears of sleeping poets and saying it as it is. Dreams also connect us to our divinity and ultimately to God. We access our spiritual connection to higher consciousness and to the divine through the crown chakra.

And so we enter the Purple Room.

The Purple Room

Access to the Purple Room is not a given. You can journey a long time and still not reach it. Or you may actually get to and spend time in the Purple Room without knowing it. Most of us have been there but do not realise it. That is what happened to me, on a wet winter night in Dublin. A group of us, soul pilgrims and students of the late Paddy McMahon, spiritual teacher and author, had gathered to work on our psychic intuitive and spiritual awareness. Paddy had initiated us into a soul journey or visualisation, accompanied by our spirit guides. The journey lasted a long time; after a while, the room faded and I stopped hearing Paddy's voice.

I found myself, after what seemed a long voyage, crossing a large majestic and crystalline bridge, entering into a large purple mansion that seemed to be suspended in the sky. Several wise beings in mauve and lavender robes appeared to be waiting for me at the entrance. Crystal lights of all colours shone from the anteroom within and I had the sense that I had been here before. Traversing the anteroom, I felt driven along by a great force until at last, I came to a wide beautiful space radiating healing energy and light. Indigo, then mauve and finally purple colours filled the space until I knew I was in the Purple Room. Awed by the force of love, energy and light around me, I hesitated, but my spirit guides smiled and guided me to sit on a large canopy draped in rich, thick tapestry. I sat and immediately three angels came and placed their hands on my body, urging me to lie down and accept their healing energy. I felt instantly at ease, peaceful, and very loved. Some long while later, accompanied by my spirit guides, I was taken to a section of the room filled top to bottom with beautiful books. Rows and rows of beautifully bound volumes stood proudly on the shelves. Scanning the books, I was drawn to one and pulled the book from the shelf – it had my name on it. As if by magic the book opened at a page. A beautiful Goddess was seated at a large table, writing. Underneath the image were the words, "Write about dreams, about how dreams are the path to our souls; write about the vastness of spiritual knowledge, love and light available to all of us; write about how we are never alone." Entranced, I was about to take up the pen and start writing when I heard Paddy's voice cut through my visualisation.

"You can come back now," he said… Then, when I didn't respond, "It's okay to come back." Reluctantly I dragged myself away from what felt like heaven, and landed again in the room with Paddy and my soulmates. There were tears on my cheeks. Everybody had been waiting for me and seemed relieved I was back. "I didn't want to come back – it is so lonely here." Paddy, gentle wise soul that he was, understood. "Our earthly challenge is to know that we are never alone," he spoke softly. It has taken a long time for me to rest in these words and learn to trust in the benevolent all-encompassing power of spirit, and to truly know that I am indeed not alone. That we are not alone, and that we have access to the divine; we have but to ask.

I take up my pen and write now. I can never do justice to the beauty, love, and magnificence of spirit I encountered in the Purple Room, but, as clinician and midwife to the soul, I can write about dreams.

Dreams: Path to your Soul

The dream is the small hidden door in the deepest and most intimate sanctum of the soul, which opens to that primeval cosmic night that was soul long before there was conscious ego and will be soul far beyond what a conscious ego could ever reach.
– CG Jung

In my late thirties, after spending some years in Jungian analysis, I decided to train as a psychotherapist. Since I had previous training in dance/drama therapy and more experiential and humanistic therapeutic modalities, I wanted a training that was broad based and not too restrictive. For me any training in psychotherapy needed to embrace the spiritual or transpersonal realm, I instinctively knew this. My previous trainings and experiences in the field of pre- and perinatal psychology together with my work as a prenatal and birth teacher had rooted in me a knowing which I needed to honour. In Jung I found something that orthodox psychoanalytic theory did not have. Jung gave the psyche wings, his archetypal theory meant that the soul could be understood for what it is: transcendent and eternal, and that being so, always open to transformation and the numinous. And that we were spiritual beings in physical form, not the other way around. This meant that any psychology had to be growth orientated rather than purely based on a medical model. In actual fact my training in psychoanalytic psychotherapy was only bearable because of Jung. I found much of classical Freudian and Kleinian psychoanalysis confining and generally unable to contain the pre- and perinatal domain, which I had understood was so much a part of my own healing journey. Having completed further study and therapeutic experiences in regression and past-life therapy, I knew that a transpersonal approach was necessary.

And then there were dreams.

Your dreams are a direct path to your soul. Dreams come to us unfiltered from our egos and are part of the language of our souls. The function of dreams is ultimately to bring things to our attention and to help us to grow. Dreams act as a regulating function in the psyche designed to increase our awareness, bring about healing and create inner balance. Additionally, dream imagery has an important function as our connector to the divine within. Far from being crazy or meaningless, dreams have a deep intelligence; they are our psyche's way of helping or guiding us on our human and spiritual path. Jung writes that, *"Dreams are the direct expression of unconscious psychic activity."*[24] Dreams are 'illuminators' into the vast contents of our unconscious, and contain riches and transformational gems set to help us become more whole. Far from simply exposing everything we repress for the sake of 'adaptation', they are compensatory mechanisms to help us see the picture from our soul's perspective and achieve inner and outer balance. By illuminating our inner life, dreams bring 'our story' to us at night, when our ego is asleep. Another quote from Jung:

> *The dream, by virtue of its source in the unconscious, draws upon a wealth of subliminal perception, and it can sometimes produce things that are very well worth knowing.*[25]

From my numerous years in Jungian analysis and of being a therapist, I know working with dreams is an important if fundamental part of the therapeutic journey. As doorway to the unconscious and indeed to the divine within, dreams are invaluable. Sometimes the images produced by our psyche in dreams become, literally, a gateway to our healing. By revealing what we have been hitherto unaware of in conscious life, dreams offer us a unique insight into our own souls. A compensatory mechanism of a self-regulating psyche, dreams have a healing power by bringing us to a more balanced psychological state. In Jung's view, the function of dreams is to promote a better adaptation to life by compensating the one-sided limitations of consciousness.

> *The psyche is a self-regulating system that maintains its equilibrium just as the body does. Every process that goes too far immediately and inevitably calls forth compensations, and without these there would be neither a normal metabolism nor a normal psyche. Too little on one side results in too much on the other. Similarly, the relation between conscious and unconscious is compensatory. This is one of the best-proven rules of dream interpretation. When we set out to interpret a dream, it is always helpful to ask: what attitude does it compensate?*[26]

Symbols and Images

The language of the soul is image and symbol. The unconscious has a rich capacity to create symbols and images, and to derive information from a pool of data far more extensive than that directly available to ego consciousness. Dreams carry treasures that enhance the meaning and depth of our life's journey. Illuminating our inner landscape, they help us come to know disowned parts of ourselves and provide guidance on our life path. The images in our dreams become metaphors we can work with to bring about change and healing in our lives. Indeed, image as a metaphor is both connector to the inner life of our soul and transformer. In other words, if we take note of and follow the images in our dream, it takes us directly to not only our own soul, but to the divine and to the healing energy we need to 'transform' our consciousness and bring about emotional balance and healing. The power of imagery to affect us is well documented. It is widely accepted, for example, that watching violent or horror films negatively affects our immune system, whereas viewing beautiful, loving films have a harmonising effect on our system. In today's technological world we are urged to put down our devices at least one hour before bed, if we want to sleep well. In fact, there is more to it than that. Our cell phones, computers and iPads bring us into the outer world with its noise, stimulation and chaos, encouraging us away from our precious inner world. Spending time with ourselves, in silence or contemplation, needs to become a vital part of our daily living if we want to be healthy and lead authentic and mindful lives.

Care of the soul includes listening to our dreams as the voice of our inner life. Marion Woodman, Jungian analyst and author, writes much on dreams and metaphor as connecter:

Once we get used to listening to our dreams, our whole body responds like a musical instrument.

And further:

The more you work with your dreams and your unconscious, and honor it, the more you understand it and it understands you. When you develop a relationship with your psyche this way, you begin to carry that energy into life and your relationships.

I see working with my dreams as soul work vital to achieving psychological balance. The relationship between the dream and the dreamer is very important – and this relationship should be kept alive as long as possible and not be interpreted away too quickly. The moments alone with one's soul are precious and should be enjoyed and respected. Most Jungians, including myself, stipulate that working with dreams means not simply writing them down, but also giving the dream imagery form through painting, drawing, active imagination and maybe bodywork. For each person, the journey will be individual and unique. The important thing is to bring the dream to life and honour it as having meaning in your life. Dreams, as a representation of our 'inside story' as it were, enable us to view things differently and with a larger perspective. Also, there is usually a thread to dreams, which when noted can reveal a psychological process unfolding.

A Sense of Balance

Dreams provide a symbolic pathway to our hidden fears and desires. It is often the case that the dream suggests in images what the conscious life lacks or needs as a way of getting back into balance. The psyche, like the body, always seeks balance, and indeed it is a state of imbalance that causes suffering or disease. Your inner voice, however, can disagree completely from what you 'think' in conscious life. Your soul will tell you the truth and bring your awareness to what you need to know. An example I often give is of a client who idolised her mother and continually insisted in therapy that her mother was wonderful, nurturing and everything a mother should be. Then one day she comes to therapy very upset because of a dream she has had the night before. Recounting her dream, my client tells me she dreamt that her mother was a prostitute and a drunk, on the edges of society. Of course we both knew this was not the case in waking life, but her wise psyche was telling her she was idealising her mother and not in touch with reality, that her mother was human, and that being so, fallible and flawed. She needed to be more balanced and accept her mother's shortcomings. This awareness in itself would free her to be available to herself and her childhood experience.

The psyche, like the body, possesses the capacity to heal

itself, and it is in the compensatory function of the unconscious that this power for self-healing resides. Dreams and particularly a series of dreams are important in that you can see in them and perceive the natural processes of healing and individuation. A vital expression of the psyche's ability to heal itself is the way in which the unconscious gives rise to symbols capable of reuniting conflicting tendencies which seem irreconcilable at the conscious level. What appears impossible in our outer life becomes possible when viewed from our inner self. Jung called this the transcendent function – he came to see that the fundamental problems in life cannot be solved, they can simply be outgrown, so that people grow beyond their problems. In fact, staying with the conflict of opposites or the polarities seems to bring us eventually to a resolution. The dream can be seen as information emanating from the darkness of the unconscious and from a field of possibilities. Jung makes it clear that one has to become aware of both poles of every conflict and endure, in full consciousness, the tension created between them; then some radical shift occurs which leads to their transcendence. The importance of this lies in the fact that there is always a possibility of reconciliation between apparently irreconcilable forces – and this knowledge can bring us wisdom (and resilience in the face of adversity).

Healing Dreams

Dreams have a great power to heal us. Healing dreams come after a while when the psyche has, if you like, reproduced the trauma over and over and is ready for healing. This often happens when the dream produces a 'new' image, signifying a healing or shift has taken place in your psyche. In the first year of my analysis, I had recurring dreams of going on a journey but always without luggage. The dream each time ended with me arriving at my destination, standing at the baggage carousel realising I had no luggage and wondering how I would manage without clothes or personal effects. In some dreams, my luggage was lost. In others, I simply didn't have any. I was anxious because I had nothing to wear except what I was standing in. After we had been working together for some time, I dreamt again that I had no luggage, but that this time I had a long black dress with buttons given to me by my analyst which was not much but which enabled me to travel. In the dream, I wore the dress and was able to go on my journey with less anxiety than before. The dream image suggested that I now had some protection. As such, my psyche had produced a 'new' image, the dress, signifying a growth in consciousness. Dresses, clothes, uniforms and so on symbolically represent the archetype of the Persona, which is a Jungian term for that part of us which has acquired the social skills to function adequately in the outside world. It was given to me by my analyst, indicating what I had gained at this point in my therapeutic journey. It meant that I had become a little stronger in myself. Instead of being vulnerable and without the resources to undertake my life journey with security, I had gained a sense of self, however small.

Thanks to Jung's work we have that wonderful gateway to the unconscious, our own and the collective, so that healing is always possible and within reach. But like entering the Purple Room, access is only granted when we seek and truly wish to know ourselves. Some people are so enthralled by conscious life that they may not give time to become aware of their inner life. And some say they do not dream. However, the likelihood is that they are not open to the unconscious or to the realm of the spiritual or the imaginal. This often changes when a person experiences a crisis in their lives such as a bereavement or becomes ill for example. We may come to a juncture in life when the outer world no longer suffices to contain or deal with our problems or preoccupations, forcing us to go within for inspiration or answers. And if we ask, or seek, the divine answers, the door opens. I love Rumi's words, *"What you are seeking is also seeking you."* In difficult times, I gain great comfort from knowing this sacred truth. I have come to trust my dreams implicitly. I've noticed that dreams appear to come more quickly and more vividly not only when we engage with them but also when we are really suffering. I have found that when I am really deeply engaging with my soul and experiencing distress and anxiety in my conscious life, my unconscious appears to speak louder. Profound experiences such as childbirth can trigger many such moments for the numinosity of dreams to come through and with it the potential for healing. Take the following – When I was working as a birth and prenatal teacher I attended many births and worked with many women before and after they gave birth. The following dream (with the permission of the dreamer) appeared in my book *Songs from the Womb*. I have decided to include it here as testimony to the incredible ability of the psyche to heal and the power of dreams.

Jackie came to me for post-natal counselling, after attending prenatal classes before the birth of her son. In her thirties, she was a mature and sensitive woman who had embarked late on motherhood. She looked forward to the birth, and whilst preparing for what she hoped would be a normal birth, she was not unduly rigid about how that should happen. Nonetheless, her labour, and the birth of her son, fell far short of what she had been expecting and caused her profound pain. At full term, she was induced with oxytocin (a labour-inducing drug) and after a long and painful labour, her son was born by the use of forceps. It was said by the medical attendants at that time that Jackie's contractions were insufficient, and that she was unable to push her baby out herself. Jackie experienced the birth as traumatic, particularly the forceps delivery. A few weeks after the birth she came to the post-natal group and asked me if I would see her privately for psychotherapy. Jackie was a naturally warm person, and it was clear to me that she had been hurt very deeply and that she badly needed to talk about her experience.

She appeared haunted and withdrawn. In the sessions Jackie 'relived' the birth a number of times, always becoming very distressed as she did so. She needed to recount her birth story over and over again, and for me to listen to it. She felt that Chris had been "taken from her", removed from her body, and that she had not been able to give birth to him. Worst of all, and compounding the pain she felt about the manner in which the birth had taken place, was her sense of guilt that her baby had been subjected to the harsh violence of the forceps. This was very painful for her and threw up all her old feelings of not being good enough. Jackie had been in analysis before and had worked on this aspect of her feelings, but giving birth had reactivated old wounds. In addition to her feeling of guilt at not having been able to give birth to Chris herself, Jackie experienced the forceps birth as personally disempowering and humiliating. The experience left her feeling profoundly violated. This was painfully illustrated by a dream, which Jackie recounted in the first session.

> There are two men fixing the roof of my house. They are rough workmen, and I bring Chris up to them to show him off. One of the men says, "May I hold him?" "Yes," I answer and hand Chris to him. The workman holds the baby and then asks, "Can my mate hold him?" He is a stern-looking man, but Chris is passed to him. I turn away, chatting to the first man. Then I hear Chris whimper, I turn round suddenly to take the baby, and when he is placed in my arms I see that the man has put his eyes out.

A powerful and deeply distressing dream. Such was the power of the imagery and emotion in the dream, it affected us both and resonated in the room long after Jackie had left. In my interpretation I considered the two workmen represented the doctors who delivered Chris. That they were rough workmen is how Jackie's unconscious experienced them. Workmen fixing the roof of her house spoke of her vulnerability and sense of being physically open and unprotected during her son's birth. That one of them put her baby's eyes out is symbolic of a deep wound to the soul. Eyes are often called mirrors of the soul, and from the Oedipus myth, we learn that eye gouging is also symbolic of psychological castration. For when Oedipus learns of his crime, he is so appalled that he puts his own eyes out, and is thus condemned to a life of blind wandering. In Jackie's dream, when her baby is returned to her, he has been blinded. The dream image is very specific, and shows us clearly that not only had Jackie (her young animus, aka her little son) been deeply wounded by her experience of giving birth, but also that she perceived how wounding it had been for her child to be born in this way. And the feeling, the emotion in a dream, Jung reminds us, is a powerful tool for the therapist to consider when working with someone. The feeling in the dream was so strong it affected me deeply, as it no doubt affected Jackie. I felt for her and understood her deep anger and sense of disempowerment by the medical team in attendance at the birth of her son. The dream, which came shortly after the birth and had been recurrent since then, ceased as a result of the therapy. And although as a Jungian I do not need reminding of the power of dreams, at times some stand out for their amazing ability to change, to enlighten, to move and to heal. For so often dreams are the soul's ways of speaking to us when we are so wounded that we cannot see. I believe that by listening to and telling our dreams to someone else and having them witnessed, we discover our inside stories. And when we have learnt the story of the soul, then it ceases to plague us by recurrent dreams or symptoms.

Lost Baby Dream

Dreams, as said, have an incredible power to heal us. Here is a dream I had some months after I lost a baby in early pregnancy. I was in analysis at the time and working through a deeply wounding experience that had triggered my original birth wound. Pregnant unexpectedly at the late age of forty-one in a marriage that was by then not working, I had initially not wanted this new child. Nonetheless, after a brief period of adjustment, I had looked forwards to this new pregnancy and been extremely distressed and suffered a great deal emotionally as well as physically during a traumatic miscarriage. One of the things that had distressed me the most was not being able to see my tiny child who would have been fully formed if minute at just over three months gestation. This feeling was compounded by insensitive and rough treatment by a doctor who told me my baby had disintegrated and that I had passed 'bits of conceptus' (medical term meaning the products of conception) and not a whole child. For weeks I talked and wept with my analyst, repeating the same things over and over. Then finally one day I had the following dream. I am in the upstairs of my parents' house and I am being shown a tiny PERFECTLY formed foetus/baby in the palm of a hand.

A profound feeling of grace and a sense of completion and wholeness accompanied the dream. Again the feeling, the emotion was very strong. I have no idea whose hand my baby had been in but I sense it was God's hand. I have no doubt this was the numinous, this was the sacred at work, this was healing. And for me a profound healing. It is like I was being gifted and told, "Your baby was/is whole and beautiful/you are whole and beautiful." My analyst too received this dream, as a numinous, sacred event.

You are Never Alone: Connecting to the Sacred

The crown chakra governs our connection to the divine, to universal consciousness and the spiritual world. As such, our Sacred Contract and information on our spiritual destiny and life plan can be illuminated through this connection. Author and spiritual teacher Caroline Myss writes:

A Sacred Contract is an agreement your soul makes before you are born. You promise to do certain things for yourself, for others and for divine purposes. Part of the Contract requires that you discover what it is that you are meant to do. The Divine, in turn, promises to give you the guidance you need through your intuition, dreams, hunches, coincidences, and other indicators.[27]

Trust in your intuitive knowing and your 'hunches' – it is likely to be your soul nudging you. In the Purple Room you will encounter your own divinity and beingness as a numinous soul. Numinous means sacred and capable of transformation. We have the ability to encounter the numinous in everyday life, and most often when we are deeply wounded and suffering. It seems that in our suffering we open a door, or rather we walk through a door the divine is always ready to open for us. The numinous is in every wound because every wound holds within itself the power of its own healing. Nonetheless, it is often hard for us to accept and understand that healing lies in the wound itself. Our wounds drive us into ourselves, and can genuinely allow us an immediate and intimate contact with our soul.

As Leonard Cohen sang, *"There is a crack in everything, that's how the light gets in."* In the search for perfection that is part of secular life, we don't believe or trust this sacred truth. Having lost touch with an essential aspect of our nature, namely the divine within, the part of us that is made of starlight and has the capacity to self-heal, we tend to look outside of ourselves for answers to our problems and to heal. This does not work; as I wrote in my last book, healing comes from within. If we can connect more often with the energies of the Purple Room (our crown chakra), through meditation or a spiritual practice specific to us, we will gradually learn to trust and to heal. My own experiences of entering the Purple Room have by now anchored in me a greater trust in the divine and my own sacred beingness. Although my faith is often sorely tested, I regularly travel there even if I have to contend with my own fear.

Nature as Connector

Fear stops many of us in our tracks. As a constant, our conscious fear has of course its function as protector. However, we may be fearful of letting go of what we know, or the security blanket of our secular lives for an uncertain and worse, unknown spiritual future. There is nothing concrete about spirit, about inspiration or illumination. There is no physical hand we can hold on to during the most perilous parts of our spiritual journey. We are urged to let go, surrender and just be, in the trusted knowledge of being held in divine arms; how hard is that? Very hard. I can only share with you what holds me, what gives me comfort and how I can 'be with' the divine and say no to fear. The sea and the earth is my Great Mother. Walking by the sea and on the land restores me to a sense of wholeness, always. As I wrote some time ago, the constancy of nature, the mountains I can see from my windows and the voice of the sea restore me gently to some place of peace and wholeness. It is as though, reconnecting with the rhythms of nature, I return to myself. Sharing myself with nature, becoming part of the heartbeat of the world, reminds me I am here and it is okay. I can lie back and let the sea hold me and allow the spirit of the earth to cradle me. And so, this is my path to the divine and to my soul.

The poet Rilke speaks of this connection when he tells the young poet that the sea *"cleanses me with its noise and lays a rhythm upon everything in me that is disturbed and confused."*[28] My dreams are my connector too, in a different way, and I will sometimes ask for a dream to help clarify my confusion. Over time and with the discipline of spiritual practices such as meditation, yoga, working with my dreams and walking by the sea, I am better at allowing myself to just be and not allowing fear to send me scurrying back to 'my box'. A box which has long become way too narrow, too confining for me. Do not be afraid to travel to your own interior, in the words of Rumi: *"Journey within yourself. Enter a mine of rubies and bathe in the splendour of your own light."*

When I stop writing I see I am now alone in the Purple Room. It is late enough, and time for me to answer the call of the sea and return to her shores. There is work for me to do.

Part Two

Healing Rooms

Chapter Nine

The Birth Room

Before I formed you in the womb I knew you,
before you were born I consecrated you.
– Jeremiah 1:5

The sea crashed onto the shore sending salty sprays high into the air. I stand on the beach as close to the edge as I can and lift my arms wide, receiving and inhaling mother nature's healing and invigorating energy. Watching the wild waves gather, swell and then crash, I immediately think about the waves of birth that come and go, bringing new life closer with each surge. I think of the aeons of women who have given birth and my own experiences of childbirth, more than thirty years ago and yet as fresh in my memory as today. I think of all those pregnant women yet to give birth and wish for them to be carried and nurtured by their own wild natures. If only we, and they, could be inspired by the Great Mother, the sea, with her natural rhythms and tides so that in giving birth we flow with our own birthing power. Sadly, I know that in many ways, modern life and the medicalisation of such initiations as birth and death have robbed us of the ancient wisdom and birth knowing deep in our bones. And I know it is part of my work to bring these teachings back so as to awaken within each of us the natural cyclical rhythms and primordial instincts we were born into. That night, still with the salt spray on my body and the sounds of the sea drifting in through my bedroom's open window, I have a dream.

I am a healer or high priestess, dressed all in white, except for the
red birth sash I tie around my waist. There are others around me;

they seem to be busy with their own essential tasks; some of them are my students. It is early in the morning on a beautiful sunny day and time to get to work. I enter one of the healing rooms and survey the scene. The smells and sounds of the room call me, in the same way as does the fresh scent of song birds and early summer mornings. There is a feeling of anticipation in the air and the strong energy of new life pulsing to be born. Inside, separated by low walled cubicles, are several women in various stages of labour. The room is large, airy and with muted light, except for the huge water pool at one end around which features even larger windows overlooking the sea. The windows are open, so that the sounds of the sea and mother nature can penetrate the room and otherwise soothe those giving birth. Some women choose to labour here in the water, returning to their own birthing cubicles to give birth. And some choose to birth outside, on the firm ground of mother earth. I know that in a while, the air will be punctuated by the first sharp cries of the newborn, and that the blood mingled smell that is unique to birth will fill the atmosphere.

This is my favourite room; the Birth Room.

I wake reluctantly from my dream and hurry along to work. It is already late morning but I feel energised and inspired. I enter the birth healing room where several women await. Some have given birth and are hurt or haunted by their experience, others are numb or depressed, finding it hard to bond with their babies, and some still await their babies but are terrified of giving birth. I make sure each woman has a gentle loving companion to assist and be with her, until she is ready to enter the healing room for her personal session. The same companion will escort her away when she is ready to return home. On entering my own healing space, I light a candle and ensure the light is soft and a loving, rose-scented energy fills the room. I meditate a few moments and call in the healing energies of the Sacred Feminine and the birth knowing of the ancients and the Goddess. The room is filled with unconditional love and a gentle healing energy. Then, one by one I ask each woman to enter the healing room, which has now become a sacred healing temple.

Pregnancy and birth are sacred archetypal events, a fact that sadly is still not totally recognised by many. Although it is twenty years since my book *Songs from the Womb* which highlighted the spiritual dimensions of childbirth was published, there is still room for improvement in how giving birth and being born is managed. Most women, in the right circumstances and if allowed to progress naturally, can give birth attended only by midwives and other women acting as doulas, or birth companions. But the vast majority today will give birth in a modern medical age where technology has largely replaced nature. Many will suffer emotionally and spiritually from this experience. And although there is a place for medical technology, a balance between it and respecting the natural process of birth still needs to be established. Respect for the human soul is not a given in modern medicine, nor is a model of healing that combines trust in nature with modern technological advances. This was the subject of my last book. At this time, two decades later, not much has changed. Women are still suffering greatly in their experience of giving birth, some, far too many, describe their experience of childbirth as traumatic. My many years as a therapist treating women emerging from birth rooms and listening to mothers' harrowing accounts of their birthing experiences has taught me of the great importance of healing such deep emotional scars, if only to mitigate their far-reaching effects. Unresolved deeply buried trauma lives on in us and can affect us negatively in many ways, psychically, physically, and emotionally. Healing is paramount to free ourselves to live soulful authentic lives.

And so, we return to the sacred temple of the birth healing room.

Fear of Giving Birth: Annie

First in is Annie, a young woman in the later stages of pregnancy. A small, neat and somehow timid girl, Annie appears to be blooming in her pregnancy except for the palpable aura of fear emanating from her eyes. Terrified of giving birth, Annie tells me she cannot focus on her birth preparation classes and thinks she will just go for an elective caesarean section. That way she will just wake up and it will all be over. She is looking forwards to the baby, but since her mother passed away a year or so ago, Annie feels without support and a strong maternal hand to hold her on this initiatory journey. No amount of birth preparation classes, reading and information on what to expect can help her understand or deal with the panic that rises in her as she approaches the birth of her baby. All women, especially first-time mothers, need to be held and supported emotionally when going through a momentous life passage such as pregnancy and birth. If a young mother does not connect with the spiritual and fierce loving energy of the Great Birth Mother through her own mother or other female that can anchor her in the ancient primal knowing of birthing, then she may flounder in the unknown. Worse, she may not trust in her own body, or imagine that she lacks the natural resources to give birth, as hundreds of thousands of women have done before her. And to those who might have been themselves born via caesarean and who fear there is no memory of natural birth in their bodies, I say that this is not so. In every woman there is a memory, an archetypal ancient knowing in their bones, of the art of birthing. What gets in the way of the direct line to the archetypal Great Mother is one's own expectations and fears, generally based on early life experience or what has been passed on from the personal mother or maternal lineage. Stories of how difficult and painful giving birth is, or dark grim tales of abandonment, trauma or worse will frequently blot out the warm, positive nurturing stories of childbirth. And although fear is a natural emotion to feel, especially in the face of the unknown, too much of it can cause problems for the labouring mother. Instead of opening and letting go, her body will contract and may block the natural process of birth.

In one of my groups I remember a young mother pregnant with her first child who told me very early on that she herself had been born by caesarean and that her mother had had all her siblings also by caesarean. She added, that although she would like to give birth naturally, she would probably end up, like her mother, giving birth by caesarean. Despite the best of intentions, this indeed proved the case. You see, we may 'think' we know what we want, but our unconscious may think something else. There may be an unconscious expectation within us that, unless made conscious, comes to be. When working with pregnant mothers in a therapeutic capacity, it is always important to get a family and life history. How is childbirth viewed in the family? How has it been experienced, especially by the woman's own mother and the women of the family? What are the pregnant woman's own expectations, fears and anxieties? What was her early life experience? How was her own birth and her mother's pregnancy with her? A lot of questions, but these can come organically within the course of a few sessions. Along with a personal and family history it will also be important to ascertain if there is anything in the pregnant mother's current life situation that may act as a block to flowing with confidence through her pregnancy and childbirth. A previous difficult birth experience may be playing on her mind, or she may feel daunted by the unknown if this is her first pregnancy. This is the case with Annie, who, because of grieving the untimely death of her mother, had no reference point or maternal hand to hold. I will work with Annie for the remaining weeks of her pregnancy and assure her of my unconditional support and encouragement. She leaves the room with the following prescription:

Go inwards, become aware of and write out fears, expectations and anxieties.

Write out her own personal early life and birth history (if known).

Keep a dream and pregnancy journal. Bring these to our sessions.

Daily meditation, invoking the childbearing wisdom of the Sacred Feminine and the Divine Mother.

Daily positive Affirmations designed to build self-confidence and trust in herself and her abilities to give birth. An example is: *My body knows how to give birth. I trust my body.*

Regular yoga-based stretching classes and relaxation/birth visualisation. Pregnancy yoga classes will open, strengthen and prepare the body for childbirth. Journeying within will help the mother to connect with her unborn child.

Prayer or energy connection to a positive maternal source in her own family/ancestry that may have passed over. This can happen during daily meditation, invoking the birthing wisdom and energies of the Sacred Feminine.

Regular therapeutic meetings with a female on whom she has projected positive mother, such as doula, therapist or midwife/counsellor.

A pregnant mother's unconscious will be very active during pregnancy, and she may be plagued by vivid dreams, flashes of insight, or irrational fears. As with all rites of passage, the psyche is triggered in a particular way so that unconscious thoughts, beliefs, hidden traumas or emotions can be brought to the surface and released so as not to block her own process of giving birth. A past experience of miscarriage or stillbirth for example may block a pregnant mother from truly opening herself to the birthing experience. Or it could be that way back in her familial history there is a trauma surrounding childbirth. Regular yoga-based stretching classes are an important way of opening and preparing the body. In the same way, daily meditation and relaxation will support the mind, ease the emotions and lift the spirit. Positive affirmations and a connection with the energies of the Sacred Feminine, through Goddesses such as Diana, Artemis, Mary, Bridget or other Deity or spiritual being can help anchor the childbearing knowing deep in the pregnant woman's psyche. Such a connection will release positive emotions that in turn will increase the expecting mother's confidence in her own ability to give birth.

Traumatised by her Childbirth Experience: Sarah

Next comes Sarah, whose experience was similar to Jackie's whom I wrote about in the last chapter. Sarah, who had spent some years trying to get pregnant, was delighted at being so and had approached her due date with positivity, having prepared well for the birth of her baby. Nonetheless, her labour, and the birth of her son, fell far short of what she had been expecting and caused her profound pain. At full term, she was induced with oxytocin (a labour-inducing drug), and after a long and painful labour, her baby was born by the use of forceps. Sarah experienced the birth as traumatic, particularly the forceps delivery. She felt disempowered and that her son had been 'torn' from her, not giving her a chance to give birth to him herself. As she entered the birth healing room it become clear to me that she had been hurt very deeply and that she badly needed to talk about her experience. Sarah appeared withdrawn, haunted and remote. I came to know that Sarah was struggling with shame, supressed anger, guilt, disappointment and a myriad of other emotions that were jammed up in her, making her unable to be truly present and to bond with her baby. In our sessions Sarah 'relived' the birth a number of times, always becoming very distressed as she did so. She needed to recount her birth story over and over again, and for me to listen to it. She felt that her son had been 'taken from her', removed from her body and that she had not been able to give birth to him. Worst of all, and compounding the pain she felt about the manner in which the birth had taken place, was her sense of guilt that her baby had been subjected to the harsh violence of the forceps. This was very painful for her and threw up all her old feelings of not being good enough. Sarah experienced the forceps birth as personally disempowering and humiliating. The experience left her feeling totally violated. Such a reaction to an instrumental and very medically managed birth is not unusual in the least. Sadly though, such a reaction is often not understood empathically. Although many would say, well, what are you complaining about, you have a healthy baby? This does not cut it for a hurt mother and does not take into consideration her deep feelings and the effects of trauma on her psyche. Healing can only take place if her emotions and hurt are taken seriously and she receives non-judgmental listening and positive unconditional love. With our regular sessions, Sarah will be able to slowly heal. She leaves the room with this prescription:

Write out a full (unedited) raw account of her childbirth experience. Writing combined with painting or drawing gives form to her unconscious and will release the heavy emotional burden carried by her heart.

Recount her birth story and have it listened to and witnessed by me. A wounded mother may have to do this several times, until somehow, her psyche digests and begins to heal. Keep a journal and account of her dreams and bring to our session.

Daily meditation invoking the healing energies of the Sacred Feminine and unconditional love of the Divine Mother.

Release and let go of the negative energies generated by such thoughts as 'being a failure', a 'bad mother' and so on. This can be done during meditation or visualisation and in session.

Daily affirmations such as: "I am a loving and good mother," or "I am a blessing to my children." Repetitive affirmations combined with meditation or prayer serve to ground the healing energies thus generated.

Attend Yoga-based or other post-natal exercise classes. Expressing how she feels in an accepting, non-judgmental environment, amongst her own peers, will be healing. Bodywork, especially yoga, helps strengthen and restore the new mother's body.

Have healing massage or other body treatments when possible, with a nurturing, motherly therapist or friend. New mothers, who have been through the initiation or ordeal of childbirth frequently, feel a little alienated from their bodies and the need for physical nurturing.

Regular therapeutic sessions can be combined with spending a little time each day being nurtured as a mother (friend cooking a meal, giving her a massage or pampering treatment).

It is the case that often and understandably, all attention tends to be given to the new baby by others. It is important to remember and spare a thought for the new mother who, whatever her experience, is likely to feel tired, hormonally emotional and at times overwhelmed. I remember being profoundly grateful to a girlfriend of mine who, after the birth of my daughter at home, called to the house and cooked several meals for us, placing them in the freezer for later use. And while other visitors and family members were downstairs chatting, she came into my room and asked me if I was hungry. I was, and she fed me. It was the best banana sandwich I have ever tasted!

Post-Natal Depression: Magdalene

Next is Magdalene who is depressed and cannot bond with her baby. A beautiful red-haired woman in her late thirties,

Magdalene comes alone to the healing room. She has left her baby girl at home with her husband, two other children and mother-in-law. After two natural births, Magdalene gave birth to her daughter by emergency caesarean section. At only thirty weeks, the little one had spent several weeks in the neonatal unit before being released and taken home. Because of complications and the prematurity of her baby, Magdalene had been unable to breastfeed her child, a fact which really affected her, she told me. Worst, however, was the feeling she could not connect with her baby. Try as she might, it seemed there was some kind of block or distance between them. Not having been 'awake' for the birth, Magdalene had a sense of strangeness, who was this child they said was hers? Again not an unusual reaction to a caesarean. I remember one young mother who ended up with a caesarean section after a long, protracted labour. She was found later roaming the wards, tears running down her cheeks, asking, "Did you see my baby being born?" Every midwife she met was asked the same question until eventually she spoke with the actual midwife who had assisted at the operation. The young mother questioned her again and again, as if by doing so each detail of the precious experience which had been denied her would be indelibly imprinted in her soul and the experience restored to her.

Many women have told me how important it was for them to actually feel or see their baby emerging from their bodies. Not being able to do this resulted for some in tremendous pain and loss, feelings of unreality and detachment, and most commonly a sense of something missing. As I wrote in *Songs from the Womb*:

Although we are unlikely to be able to obliterate the need for caesarean section births, awareness of the psychological implications, as well as the sensitivities of the mother and her baby, should encourage better handling of this important event. A recognition of the emotional effects of surgical intervention on the experience of birth, would enable the procedure to be conducted as humanely as possible, with special regard for the sanctity of birth and the importance of bonding between mother and child.[29]

Separation of mother and baby at a time when it is crucial that they be together is compounded by the mother's reaction of detachment from a baby she has difficulty believing came from her. Many women who have had their babies by caesarean feel that there is something missing. Others feel cheated out of something and some feel profoundly depressed, but are unable to say why. Even more devastatingly, deep feelings of insecurity and negative self-image are common, as the mother blames herself for being unable to do what other women do so naturally.

It is true to say that women often unconsciously see giving birth as a test of their womanhood and so women whose babies are delivered by caesarean section (and often, forceps) can suffer from a negative self/body image after the birth, since they feel their bodies were unable to function normally. Such women carry a sense of wounded feminine pride. This feeling can run very deep and take a while to uncover and heal. I have worked with many a wounded mother who carries a profound sense of guilt, that in some way she has deprived her child of the experience of normal birth, something which many consider to be a birthright. Talking with Magdalene, it was clear that, guilty at having inflicted pain on her baby, she was somehow punishing herself and her body, which, as she saw it, had let her down so badly. Difficulty bonding with a baby who seems like a stranger, she feels disconnected from her baby and therefore from part of herself. She feels guilty that she should feel so bad about the experience; after all, she has a healthy baby, so what has she got to be so miserable about? She fears that no one will understand her feelings; she is in mourning for something, she is not sure what. She is grieving for the loss of her ideal birth.

Feeling that she will not be understood, she turns inwards into her pain and sense of shame; she becomes depressed and unable to cope, which in turn causes more guilt and she develops post-natal depression.

It is also true that oftentimes, such an experience of giving birth may additionally trigger past hurts, traumas or unresolved issues in the new mother's past. Such material will be pulled to the surface of her psyche; as she struggles to deal with her own experience, she (re)experiences previously unmetabolized or unintegrated soul pain. Magdalene tells me her own mother had experienced prolonged bouts of post-natal depression, resulting in several stays in hospital. As a child feeling abandoned and fearful, Magdalene has painful memories of her mother being taken away by ambulance and of her terror at not knowing if she would see her mother again. I will work with Magdalene weekly for as many weeks as are needed. Magdalene leaves the healing room with the following prescription:

Go inwards, become aware of, and write out fears, anxieties and her deepest feelings about the birth of her daughter. Some of these undigested feelings may go back to childhood. These can be discussed in personal sessions.

Write out her personal life history, including her early life and own birth history (if known), including her relationship with her mother.

Take note of and keep a dream journal and bring to sessions. Dreams will reveal what is going on in her psyche and largely determine our work going forwards.

Daily meditation invoking the healing sacred energies of the Feminine and Divine Mother.

Daily body healing visualisation and release of negative thoughts such as, "I am a bad mother," or "My body has failed me." Focusing on bringing light into her chakras especially the root and sacral chakra along with her uterus will help her body heal and feel loved.

Daily affirmations such as, "I am held in the arms of the Divine"; "I am a good and loving mother"; "My body has done a good job." These can be done, along with prayer when invoking the unconditional love and healing energies of the Sacred Feminine and Divine Mother.

Regular attendance at post-natal exercise or yoga groups to strengthen and restore both body and mind post childbirth.

Spend time each day nurturing herself as a mother with a loving healing ritual (need not be more than 20 minutes).

Holding Hands with the Birth Goddess

When the Womb is Healed
And Reconnected to the Heart
Sacred Woman Will Stand in her Power
– Christine Page

One of the most important if not vital elements of healing is the feeling of being held. No amount of 'words' or analysis or talking or listening will heal. Healing comes from the much more subtle area of the heart. A person senses when he or she is being emotionally 'held'. In my own therapeutic experience, I know that a feeling of empathy, of connection between myself and the other person is vital to emotional healing. Nowhere is this more important or necessary than in healing birth. Pregnant and birthing women are particularly vulnerable and 'open' and need, consciously or unconsciously, the embodied love of the Mother. And I mean embodied. It is Mother who gives life and nurtures it. This is why I have added to my birth healing prescription regular time with a 'mother' surrogate such as healer/therapist/midwife or counsellor who will personify the positive nurturing Mother. Sometimes a family member such as a grandmother will be able to embody the unconditional loving energies of the mother archetype but of course it is not a given and very much dependent on the relationship a client has with her family. Suffice it to say that a big open heart, unconditional loving and being comfortable inhabiting those 'secret places' I wrote about earlier is an integral part of healing. In my own life as a therapist, I am thinking now of the many beautiful strong women and mothers that came to me after the birth of their babies, broken in both body and mind with nothing to bind them together except their pain and tears. Some were numb, their trauma buried in the tissue and cells of their bodies. But they came and were able to hold their pain up to me for safekeeping until it felt safe enough to inhabit their bodies again. And to hold their head high and find their voice. For my part, truly being there with my heart open, inviting the Divine Feminine into the room created the sacred space we needed. As a therapist, having long ago abandoned the analytic 'blank screen' persona taught to us in our training and allowing myself to be moved, I sometimes cried with my clients. I found this only brought us closer and reinforced a much needed and therapeutic bond.

Birthing, pregnancy and childbirth is a deeply embodied archetypal process inhabiting all parts of us women in a visceral way. For some of us it is an amazing journey into the deep feminine mysteries and an opportunity to inhabit our spirituality in a profoundly unique way. At the same time, childbirth brings us into the realm of the Goddess and the collective experience of all women that have given birth before us. And although modern medicine and the advances of modern life have arguably made birth safer, deep in our psyches we know women have died in childbirth, and we intuitively know we are entering a rite of passage, an initiation. Journeying into the unknown or the underworld is part of all sacred initiations. The ancient Celts referred to these journeys as *Immrama*, or mystical journeys.[30] These journeys can be initiated through universal human experiences such as birth and death, loss of a loved one, severe physical illness and so on. For many women, the experience of pregnancy and birth will awaken a profound sense of kinship with all women throughout history who have ever gone through this initiation.

When I work with pregnant and birthing women, the mother in me holds hands with the birthing Goddess to create an energetic line to the archetypal earth mother. In my early years as a birthing partner and prenatal teacher (before the days of doulas), I remember vividly one such occasion. Amal and I had been working together for some months as she prepared for the birth of her first child. Amal had been attending my regular yoga-based antenatal classes and was keen to have a natural birth. As she and her husband had chosen to give birth in hospital and requested I accompany them as 'doula', I was present during the birth of their son. I remember that towards the end of a fairly long labour, when her contractions were nearing their peak, Amal, clearly exhausted and uncomfortable on the hospital bed, turned to me (I was holding her hand) and begged me to tell her what to 'do'. Her eyes pleaded for help but before I could say anything she had flipped over onto all fours to ease the pain and ride through her contraction. It seemed to me in that instant that without words, through the connection between us, I was reaching down to connect with the ancient birthing wisdom of all women with a direct line to the Great Mother. I cannot explain what happened except to say that I felt we were truly accompanied by a great maternal force and wisdom. There was an energy exchanged between us which propelled her forwards somehow so that Amal gave birth shortly afterwards. In my book *Songs from the Womb* I write about how important it is that pregnant and birthing women are able to connect with a 'wise woman' or other woman on whom she can project 'positive mother'. Doing so will bring her confidence and trust in the natural process of childbirth and also her own innate abilities to undertake this initiation and rite of passage. I myself remember being very attached to the community midwife who had attended the birth of my daughter at home. In the days that followed the birth, I would eagerly wait for her daily visits so I could talk to her about everything that was going on, how I was feeling, how the baby was doing and so on. Her visits helped me feel nurtured and safe.

It has been a long day. The sun is low as I gratefully head for and enter the yoga and meditation room. Inside this sanctuary, I give thanks for the healing energies of the Great Mother and pray that all of my women will receive the warm glow of love and be surrounded by divine grace as they gradually open themselves to be healed. I know how vital it is that new mothers are given the space and encouragement to open their hearts and receive the fierce love and divine nurturing they need. As with all of us, we are not islands, we are inextricably linked and nowhere more so than a mother and her child. That being so, what is not healed or brought to consciousness in the mother will be carried by her child. Because, as in the words of sacred poet Rumi below, as spiritual beings in material form, we come to birth to fulfil our soul's destiny. And what is left undone will continue as we take our part in the eternal book of life. I think of the words of Rumi:

"We search this world for the great untying of what was wed to us at birth and gets undone at dying."

And that being so, I prepare to enter one of the other healing rooms.

Chapter Ten

The Life Room

There is a Life-force within your soul, seek that life.
There is a gem in the mountain of your body, seek that mine.
O traveller, if you are in search of That
Don't look outside, look inside yourself and seek That.
– Rumi

I remember when I first started learning the key lesson of looking within. Like most of us, my seeking tended to be focused outside of myself for a whole range of things, health, healing, happiness and love. I guess by choosing to attend a Jungian analyst for regular psychotherapy sessions I had already signed up to the idea that emotional and soul healing essentially comes from within, and that looking outside of ourselves for fulfilment is ultimately destined to fail us. But however much we might logically 'know' something, our feelings and our ego may not agree. During a difficult period in my life and railing against what I experienced as my absent or flawed emotional holding as a child, I was more than dismayed when my analyst gently suggested that I needed to pick up my little distressed child self and nurture her. *"Hold her close to your heart and love her."* What good is that, I thought, I need 'you' (or someone else) to hold me. Of course it is natural that the child part of us will surface every now and again and demand to be met. Nonetheless, my years in therapy taught me to nurture myself, however slowly or painfully that knowing came.

Another memorable learning came for me some time later, in my very early years as a therapist. A client of mine, a grown professional man of mature years, was learning to look after and nurture his inner child. He had come to me to deal with what he considered to be seminal to his healing journey, his birth, prenatal and very early life. In the course of our work together, although extremely busy by day, Patrick told me that every evening he would pull from his wallet a picture of himself as a young boy. He would talk to his young self and say, *"I'm sorry I haven't spent time with you today, but I haven't forgotten you, I love you, and I promise to spend longer tomorrow talking with you."* I remember being moved and impressed by this. If only we could all remember the importance of talking to our inner child. From my studies in energy medicine, conscious awareness, and spiritual healing, I understand that talking to and loving our bodies, our organs, and even our cells, is a powerful healing tool. Similar to affirmations, healing happens through our thoughts and through the energetic power of love to transform negative belief systems. Positive life-affirming thoughts, words and vision are a necessary part of healing. In my last book I wrote about healing from within. And about how ultimately, it is our sense of separation, or of looking for answers outside of ourselves that is the cause of our suffering. When that happens, the great life force within remains unsought and unknown. In the words of Rumi, we must seek that life.

But that learning came later. Before this, I was to experience perhaps the greatest emotional challenge of my life. A heartbreak that served as a huge awakening to love and to spirit. It was through my relationship with my late soulmate that I entered the deepest part of the ocean and my soul. And learnt the true nature of love and of life that is not designed to be smooth but rather undulated by peaks and troughs intended as soul character builders. I learnt that how you deal with what life throws at you matters more than what actually happens. Most of all, I learnt how patience and perseverance is needed to allow the gradual unfolding of a destiny and the making real of a dream. That you can meet your soulmate and know immediately you are meant to be together even if it is to ultimately shatter your heart to its expansion. And that your struggles gradually weave themselves into a pattern that eventually reveal the story of your life and your soul contract. It is twenty years since my love and I parted but the legacy of this time is witnessed in my writings and dream journals. Surely a time of heart, of soul searching, of great joy and immense pain and endurance, but also of expansion and evolution. I experienced a vast soul growth and reached a deeper place in my heart during those years. It is through our enduring soul connection, extending far beyond his physical death and the boundaries of time and space that I have come to know the divine nature of love. My spiritual growth and awareness took a giant leap at this time. Such expanded consciousness awakened me to the sacred and to the spiritual realm in a very embodied way so that since that time I have never again doubted that we are spiritual beings connected to the divine. I have never again doubted that love transcends all boundaries and is not confined to our life in physical form.

That being said, in between periods of calm and of joy, much of our time physically together felt like a love divided, as though we were both sailing the seas on different ships bound for shipwreck. In myself, I experienced intense inner turmoil as I struggled to navigate the choppiness of an angry sea. The same sea mirrored the conflict between my ego and my soul. As the sea became choppier, my ego screamed louder. Wanting to 'fix', to 'do', to condemn, to judge, I fought against the tide and went down screaming. The only respite for my bruised soul came at night in my dreams.

A Love Divided

It had been a difficult few weeks and I had grown tired of the gut-wrenching feelings of loss and loneliness. My lost love and life partner, heavy and burdened by his own demons, had taken refuge in his work and shut down communication. Walking by the sea was my only respite from the endless gnawing of my soul, so that I took to sitting on the shore for long periods of time. And gradually, as the long summer edged towards autumn, a healing began to weave itself into my soul and fill my dreams by night. One night, after walking the beach and thinking of my love, I had the following dream.

'T' and I had gone to a house together, I think it was his house, or a holiday cottage he used sometimes. The outside walls were freshly painted blue and the rooms inside were quite bare of all but essential furniture. The house was cottage like, and stood alone, surrounded by nature. 'T' was showing me around and we came to two rooms, each with its own open fire. It struck me as strange that both fires were lit and burning gently. He shows me to a single bed and says, "This is your bed, I am in the next room." Each room had a single bed. Leaving the door open, he tells me he will be next door for now, but that the door was open if I needed anything, and that the fire will keep me warm. 'T' goes to the next room after settling me in. There is a sense (perhaps he tells me) that because of what has happened in his past he has chosen to sleep next door for now but that this would pass in time, hence the open door.

The dream was so vivid and strong I can still smell the blue paint and sense the warmth of the two fires. The cottage is still so clear. I knew my partner had had some painful emotional experiences before he met me, and that in his own words, he had 'built a wall' around himself. *"I'm quite comfortable behind this wall,"* he had told me. *"It won't always be that way,"* he had added, indicating that he needed time. I know the dream was telling me about our relationship, and most clearly, about T's psyche, his 'house'. Quite clearly, my own psyche had revealed how for now, being two singles, side by side, was all that was available but that in time the situation would change. The door was open. The fires in both rooms indicated passion was alive for us both but that he was not yet able to join me in a double bed, a 'coniunctio': the love partnership I craved. And since in dreams and in love our partners usually mirror a part of us, the dream also made clear it was the same for me. My psyche told me clearly the door was open, and that both rooms had a burning fire. Clearly too, I was being shown T's house – where he was at. I was being urged to give it time, a sentiment he himself often voiced, but in those days my passion was high and I had not yet learnt the spiritual qualities of trust and patience. Regrettably, the combination of my impatience and his lack of willingness to move forwards and deal with his own blocks to intimacy drove us to an end.

Dreams point us to what we haven't been able to see thus far and come at appointed times to alter our ego consciousness in the service of wholeness and of healing. My soul showed me clearly the situation as it was, but life also has to be lived, and at that time, I was on a vessel bound for a shipwreck that was set to become a learning path on my life journey. Who can say that were I to have heeded my dream and stepped back from trying to make our relationship what I wanted it to be at that time that it would not have floundered? No one, for with what I since have come to know, the book of life and our soul destiny simply needs to be lived. My love and I had had many past lives together as is common with twin souls and soulmates. And perhaps it was not our destiny this time around to be together for life, and for his to end at a relatively young age.

The Life Healing Room

Glancing at the clock I see that it is already late but that if I hurry I will still have time for a quick walk on the beach before I need to head to work. My heart still resonating with the memories of love and of riding the tides of life; I need to be near the sea for a short while. Despite the sun peering out of a growingly cloudy grey sky there is a small breeze which promises to rise sharply as the morning wears on, so I need to hurry. I reach the group of rocks I often sit at and which offer shelter from the wind. Pulling my wool scarf closely around my neck, I sit and gaze out to sea. After a while, I close my eyes and listen to the rhythmic ebb and flow of the waves as a slow settling drops into my heart and quietens my breath. I stay like this for a short time allowing all that is jagged in me to settle quietly. I ask for help and guidance from the Great Mother for my work in the Life Healing Room. Life, as we have seen and know, is not a smooth straight path and many of us will seek help in navigating the sharper peaks and troughs. I know that the path of love is rarely straight and that today I will meet fellow soul pilgrims who come for help and healing.

A Conflict of the Heart: James

Your task is not to seek for love, but merely to seek and find all the barriers within yourself that you have built against it.
– Rumi

First in is James. A handsome man in his early fifties, James radiates charismatic energy and humour. Although generally tastefully dressed, I can see that his well-worn Levi's and faded black leather jacket had known better days, and I wonder if his work and therefore his earnings are suffering from the bouts of depression indicated in his notes. Despite being a talented graphic designer, it seems James had had a chequered career and at times has struggled to find work. Perhaps his lack of discipline and desire to be 'forever young' was catching up with him, he self-deprecatingly tells me. Always a free spirit, James had a phobia of being 'tied down' and so often changed work, preferring to be self-employed. At times he had sold cars which he bought used and revamped. Classic cars were his favourite. He had owned one during better days and even had taken part in racing rallies. Now, having fallen on hard times, he had had to part with his precious vintage car and had to contend with reviewing and writing about them for several publications. Always the life and soul of the party, James loved nothing more than being with an admiring group of people. Drawn to money and the 'good' life, he felt his lack of finances keenly. He still had a family to cater for which served as both a brake on his desire for travel and lavish lifestyle, and a drain on what money he did manage to earn, he said. And then there were the black moods he could slip into and which lately had grown more frequent, interfering with his life and no doubt putting years on him, tarnishing his rugged good looks and the polished image he liked to project.

"Why are you here?" I asked him. *"I need to sort myself out,"* he says and looks down, but not before I glimpse a restiveness descending like a dark cloud on his fair head. Looking up at me intensely from dark green eyes, James tells me he is in trouble, he needs to change. I am struck by the despairing look in his eyes. He cannot go on as he is. I encourage him to continue, to tell me more. James was fed up with love, or more accurately, with relationships. A gregarious man of wit and humour, James loved his friends. He loved his hobby, motor racing, and enjoyed being able to travel, on a whim, to one or other event. Since his divorce, James had savoured his freedom, but that was already some years ago and he still had not managed to 'settle down' with a good woman, he recounts. Having no trouble attracting women, James had many, but none of them lasted. The women, sometimes younger than him, were all of the same ilk, physically beautiful and seemingly carefree. They often had money or came from moneyed backgrounds and James was attracted by that. However, since they usually fell madly in love with him, after a while, they wanted more. Much more. The more they wanted from him, the more James retreated. Inevitably, the relationships, based as they were on somewhat

superficial values, floundered. The problem was that James himself or a deep part of him wanted more too. He just didn't trust himself, and if the truth were told, he was frightened of love. Sometimes he regretted his past relationships, which had served to make him wary of love, and sometimes, more often now, he was lonely.

"Lonely?" I enquire.

"Yes. I'd like to know why, and what is the source of my black moods."

"What happens to you when you enter your black mood?"

James tells me he stays home, emerging only to go to work if he has work, doesn't talk to anyone and just 'broods'. He feels trapped, paralysed and full of self-doubt. Despite having friends, he doesn't feel able to talk to them. But it's the guilt that gets to him the most. With a Latin background, family values are paramount he explains. Families stick together, and even though divorces happen, they are never easy since no one ever lets go. The father is patriarch and expected to provide for his children well past their childhood. Guilt is piled on the one who leaves or abandons the nest. Any new person attempting to enter the family will not be offered an easy ride. His own children, now well into their twenties, still make huge emotional and financial demands on him, which in essence, James feels unable to refuse. He knows he is being emotionally blackmailed but he feels powerless to do anything about it. He feels guilty and he's not sure why since his children, bar the youngest, were all over eighteen when he left. When his marriage had split, being short of money, he had moved in with his mother – a move he regrets and which his latest partner had called regressive. Now, his mother is edging into late old age and he wonders whether he will simply end up being her live-in carer. He feels guilty about that too, not wanting to be 'tied down', but feeling an obligation or duty of care. It seems that whatever way he looks, the noose is coming closer. James has several brothers and sisters but he is the only one that has 'fled the coop' or tried to. And been punished for that act of family 'betrayal'.

It is all a tangled mess, he tells me. On the one hand, he seeks his freedom and longs to be free of the family to live his own life; on the other, his guilty conscience and the emotional blackmail of his family pull him back. And all this has now come to a head. *"Oh?"* I interject and encourage him to say more. Well, just a few weeks ago he met a woman whom he considers *"the love of his life."* The one he has been waiting for. He knew this, deep in his heart and soul. A woman from another culture and country. But she is his soulmate, that he knows, and not like any woman he has ever met before. It's the call of his destiny, he says. This is his chance to live the authentic life his soul is pushing him to live. They had projected plans to live a simple life together in the land of her birth, where he himself had long wanted to go and where he has ancestral links. But, well, his family don't approve, he would have to leave behind all that he knows, and he is frightened. Since his new love left to go back home after their time together, he is torn. He feels the black clouds approaching again, he has started brooding and turning inwards. There is a part of him feels he is drowning. He wants help.

I am touched by his honesty and see that James is truly in touch with his heart, but the call from his soul to live a larger life brings with it difficult choices. He will need to deal with his familial complexes and whatever is pulling him back. Making hard choices is perhaps the most difficult thing to do and yet it is the mark of a man (or a woman). It is part of growing up. I myself have lived long enough to know that the ties that bind us are never easily cut. No matter how far you may travel away from those 'ties', the complicated bundle of unresolved knots will follow you. You will not be free until you deal with these knots, painstakingly unravelling them. I ask James if he is happy to meet with me again and he indicates he is. I suggest he keep a journal and pay attention to his dreams – if he can catch them. A creative man, James seems happy with this suggestion. He has actually taken to writing stories, he tells me. I smile and tell him that yes I can help him, but that in essence it is he who must heal himself. James nods, and rising from his chair, I notice that some of his buoyant, charismatic self has returned. He leaves the room with his prescription:

> Weekly sessions designed to help him find a space where he can be himself and open up about his life, his feelings and the complexes that still employ him. I get the sense that deep down, James doesn't like himself too much. Self-acceptance and love are always part of healing, but achieving these take time.
>
> I invite James to spend some time every day either meditating or simply being with himself. This may take the form of a silent meditation or else simply enhanced awareness or 'mindfulness' whilst carrying out his daily tasks.
>
> I encourage James to write his stories. It is often through the stories we create that we reveal our inner life to ourselves. I will ask him to write about himself, creating whatever characters come to mind. And since much of his difficulties and blocks are connected with his family, I will encourage him at a later date to write letters to his family, as a way for him to let go and forgive. None of these letters need to be actually sent, they are designed rather to help him clear any toxic energies that might be holding him back.
>
> To avoid the common pitfall of over analysis or 'going into the head', I suggest James take some time, if possible every day, to do some physical exercise. Yoga doesn't appeal to him, but he loves nature, he told me. Even a short walk will not only ground him but connect him with his instinctual, earth nature.
>
> With a stated tendency to overdependence on stimulants such

as alcohol and coffee, I'll invite James to simply be mindful of what he ingests. I know that this simple awareness often results in being able to reduce said stimulants. Additionally, it often happens that as we increase our self-awareness and expand our consciousness, we become more sensitive to our body and what it needs to stay healthy.

I sigh as I leave the room later that day. Thinking about it, the stories I hear and bear witness to in the Life Healing Room all sound very familiar. I have lived through some of it myself. I think of the words of many philosophers, *"Life is not a problem to be solved, but a mystery to be lived."* Yes, I think, and add under my breath, *"And our task is to live it with spiritual elegance."* As I sit on the bench in the garden having a late lunch, I feel the rustle of paper in my pocket, and half standing, I take the paper from my pocket. I had forgotten it was there. Recognising what it is, I realise I have forgotten to post it. I had been writing stories for some time, now perhaps I had a chance of being published. I take it out and read it. Perhaps it will inspire me in my work with fellow soul pilgrims in the Life Healing Room. Strange I should find it after seeing James this morning. Familiar indeed.

A Wild & Stormy Night

It was a wild and stormy night and Magda was worried. And it wasn't just about the possible disastrous effects of the bad weather on her impending journey. After all, planes took off and landed in all sorts of weather nowadays. A seasoned and experienced traveller, Magda's unease came she knew from deep inside her, and it had been there for some time. A grumbling discomfort somewhere in her gut, after her last phone conversation with Richard, had turned now into a full-blown indigestion. Something was wrong, very badly wrong. She could feel it and smell it. And she was angry with herself. She should have heeded the big red warning flags that had appeared over the last weeks. Flags that were now an almost regular appearance, particularly where the presence of her new love's family were concerned. Despite the beautiful memories she still held of their three days together in New Orleans almost three months ago, Magda had begun to have doubts about their relationship. If you could call it that – a love affair that had started to take root and was now a potentially hazardous road that love-starved Magda had started to walk. It wasn't that she hadn't had her fair share of love affairs; it was more that she had, as yet, failed to find the right soulmate to share her life with. Richard seemed to be a kindred spirit who had been alone for some time. He had been waiting for her he said. Meeting at the airport for the first time, the two lovers had quickly fallen into a fairy-tale romance leading goodness knows where. They were enchanted with each other; a magical happening took hold of them, just as soon as they clapped eyes on each other. A romantic soulful man, Richard had charmed and wooed Magda with emails, phone calls and even red roses sent to her hotel room prior to their physical meeting. His card with the words, "We are almost there," pinned to the roses, had peered out at her, filling her hotel room with the intoxicating scent of romance.

Their meeting and union had been romantic and soulful and everything both had dreamed of. After three sun-filled days of music and love, they had parted and returned to their individual lives on different continents, but not before some firm plans for a life together were made. Now, and increasingly as the pressures of his life gained momentum, to Magda's consternation, Richard's easy-going façade was beginning to crumble. She wondered who this hot-headed Latin man was who went into a sulk if he did not speak with her every day and whose protestations of love were tinged with the slightest hint of paranoia. Where was she when he phoned and didn't get her? he barked. Who was she with? A slightly aloof Magda, who needed a lot of space to feel safe, recoiled at this. She felt smothered by him. Surely a couple of times a week is enough to speak to one's loved one. After all, being more at home with her pen than with her voice, she emailed him a lot more than he did her. He preferred talking. But was *he really genuine?*

An outwardly charming and easy-mannered man, Richard's smooth-talking self disappeared with lightning precision when he felt threatened. He was quickly roused to anger and would flare up at the slightest provocation, which could just as quickly disappear. But he was in love and wanted Magda, and he must have her. Inventing all sorts of crazy scenarios when he didn't hear from her to assuage his fears, he punished her with scalding words or cold withdrawal. A man who liked to be in control, his slumbering abandonment complex had been awakened by love and was alive and kicking, no doubt propelling him along an equally dangerous road. He NEEDED to talk to her, and she should be there and waiting. Growing up in a macho culture where men controlled women, Richard couldn't help himself. And besides, he felt vulnerable living so far away from her, and had never loved or had a relationship with a European woman before. She was a stranger to him – or so he thought.

Magda had at first been flattered, then surprised, and then concerned at her lover's need to talk with her every day, several times a day, even. All the more so, she hated the way he would talk with her on his cell phone and repeatedly interrupt the conversation to talk with someone at work or elsewhere who might be demanding his attention. She felt this to be disrespectful and told him so. He didn't like that. Everyone in the US used their cell phones and spoke on them wherever, whenever. And if he didn't like her questioning of him, he would not call her for several days and then plead ignorance. His phone was lost, his daughter needed help; he had left his phone at her house and on and on. She knew he was lying, like she also knew and felt he had demons and family spectres he wouldn't share. That he was carrying some huge guilt complex around his family and his children. And ever since his grown-up children had come to stay with him over the recent holidays, he had become even more evasive and controlling.

He was not sure of her and the more he pushed the more she pulled away, feeling claustrophobic. Smothering, was how she felt it to be, along with his constant exhortations on the amazing qualities of his *daughters, to whom he had sent pictures of their time together in New Orleans. He had emailed them the day he returned with pictures of his new 'love'. That was the first red flag. There is something not quite right here she had thought. Is he looking to his daughters for their approval? Of course, long distance relationships have their pitfalls, she knew that, and not really a good way to learn about someone. An accomplished charmer and competent salesman, Richard was shiny, well-presented and silver tongued – the type of man most mothers would love! But where was she heading, what was she getting in to?*

Now, on the eve of her trip, with her case packed and her passport ready, Magda was in turmoil. The phone, abandoned on her bed, still reverberated from his last call. One hour they had spent talking, or mostly it was a distraught Richard who had done the talking, he longed to see her, all was well, but his daughter had had one of her tantrums and kept him awake all night. Of course, he didn't call it that, he said she was having a crisis of confidence. Upset that she had been misplaced by her father's new love, and complaining that no one cared about her, she had filled him with fears and guilt. Magda had picked all this up from their conversations over time, which featured as leading characters his family and this daughter in particular. She had tentatively voiced her concern and hoped that they would have time together to consolidate their relationship. After all, they (Richard and she) had only been physically together three days; not long for a couple that had already declared themselves in love and were planning a future. But Richard had prevaricated. No, it is not what you think, he had protested, she (his daughter) is just going through a hard time. And of course we will have time together, just maybe a dinner with the girls, somewhere in downtown Tampa. Don't worry, he said, but poor Marcella was feeling no one cared about her. And he had to reassure her.

Richard was sweating. It was mid-afternoon in Florida and he had not slept the night before. Waking his daughter asleep on a pull-out in the living room, he left for work at 8am and returned at lunchtime to make the bed and prepare the apartment for Magda's arrival that evening. He was nervous, he wanted to give a good impression and was longing to see Magda again and introduce her to his life and to his family. But he was worried. Marcella had gone to stay at Joanne's less than graciously. A good father, who tried to do his best, Richard had entertained his children who had come to spend the holiday period for the last two weeks and had little time to himself. The truth was, his children and his family had been, up to now, his life, and he had never managed to build one for himself. Now, after meeting Magda, he had a chance to finally live for himself, be himself, and enjoy his own life and love. Captivated, he had invited Magda to visit him in Florida. Unfortunately, Magda's arrival overlapped with Marcella's departure by four days, but he felt he had done his duty, why shouldn't he have some time now with his new love? Richard sighed. Why couldn't everyone be happy with everyone?

Richard sighed again; he was nervous. Despite his sunny demeaner, he was a man consumed by ghosts – a haunted man in many ways. Richard hated ghosts and never entertained them even though they filled his inner life. His family suffocated him as did his guilt but – no one must know this, least of all himself – he was a man that shone, a man who existed to please others. He loved his family and loved his mother, a formidable octogenarian who still had a hold over him. It is not that he put himself last, it was rather more that he didn't know who he really was. He just knew that he was drawn to Magda because she was 'outside' of all he had known before and the young free man in him wanted to live. And dance with his new love. He wanted a new life, an authentic life where he could be himself. And he knew that she wanted to dance with him too but that she had grown increasingly anxious that their nuptial bed was crowded. Marcella would have to calm down; he would make it up to her, send her home with money and the promise of another paid trip to the US with her boyfriend.

Magda scowled, and picking up one of her shoe bags, threw it at the bed. Richard had spoken bullshit; he was in denial of what was glaringly obvious. He was going to have to grow up and say it as it was and stop the conspiracy of denial because a woman like Magda would sniff out any demons of that sort. Impatient now and angry with herself that she had allowed the situation to get this far, Magda's realisation that she had walked into a trap frightened her. Oh God, not again, she groaned. Must my profession follow me everywhere, even into the bedroom? I don't want to get involved in this. Family therapy, that's what it was or would soon be if she kept this going. But what was she supposed to do now, cancel her trip? She'd been planning this time in South America for some months and had already rented an apartment for the six weeks she would spend in Buenos Aires. A flash of lightning drew her to her bedroom window to peer at the wildness outside. Rain pelted against the glass leaving large droplets stuck to the windowpane as though clinging for life in a dark and alien world. She was angry, like the raging wind, and totally fed up. She had planned this trip a long time and now it seemed something sinister was afoot. What was going on? Turning she surveyed her large half-packed suitcase, and the assortment of clothes strewn around her bed that still had to make it to the case. Colourful tango shoes lay nestled in their black bags and winter woollies jostled for space with cotton summer skirts and T-shirts. She was leaving for two months and would be travelling to different parts with varying climates.

She was angry and disappointed. A psychologically educated woman with a girl's heart she was no stranger to guilt herself, only she had grown accustomed to confronting those very demons and knew somewhere that awareness, although painful, also brought with it the chance of redemption. Ghosts can only be released from their hold if we acknowledge them. Otherwise they live through us. And who was she to interfere in a middle-aged man's family story? Perhaps he had done something terrible in his youth, perhaps he felt he owed his children, perhaps even he felt unworthy of a life of his own. Who knows? Magda only suffered and lamented the fact that she had been caught up in his struggle. Why couldn't it just be easy? Already Richard had revealed he had little or no money (all he had he gave to his children she was later to find out) and that with his ties to them and his job, it would be she that would do the travelling – alone. For now, the free-spirited

Magda was happy to comply – she loved travelling, but she wasn't sure she wanted to spend time with her lover's troublesome daughter. Or become embroiled in father-daughter jealousy and dynamics. But surely Richard at middle age should be able to handle his daughter?

What a mess. Magda suddenly felt this was all a dreadful mistake; should she cut loose now, change her flight and go directly to Buenos Aires, where she had planned some time? Two months in vibrant Buenos Aires dancing the tango and learning Spanish, travelling to Patagonia and the South Pole maybe. Give up on Richard; give up on love. But almost as quickly as it came, her despondency and anger made way for her plucky adventurous self. How exciting was this? Meeting a lover on the other side of the world, different culture, different life than the one she had entertained in her homeland for some time now. Always an adventuress at heart, Magda loved travelling and was attracted to foreign men. Falling for a stranger, every time. Perhaps she would write a book about this one day. And besides, she was already attached to Richard, mad about him really, and who can give up on a chance of love, even if it is on the daring side?

Wherever you are and whatever you do, be in love.
– Rumi

Chapter Eleven

The Death Room

Give sorrow words;
The grief that cannot speak
Whispers the o'er frought heart
And bids it break.
– *Macbeth* IV.111, Shakespeare

Death is something most human beings find very difficult. Although some cultures celebrate death in ritual practices such as the Mexican Day of the Dead (El Día de los Muertos), most cultures and individuals approach death, dying and endings with some degree of trepidation, emotional paralysis or fear. Additionally, our modern medicalised ethos of sanitizing birth and death have not helped us deal with such initiations in a natural, heartfelt or soulful way. Death is part of life and as such an integral aspect of our human journey. In my own life and through my many experiences of loss, I know how important it is to "give sorrow words": to allow yourself to mourn and to open your heart to bereavement. Faced with perhaps unbearable emotions around death and endings, it is tempting to batten down the hatches, close your heart and escape into a welcomed anaesthesia. Anaesthesia can come in many forms, overwork, compulsive addictive behaviour, over spiritualisation, dependence on drugs and alcohol to name some. However, to unlock the doors of your grief and allow the energy of anguish to emerge is both healing and soul strengthening. I have felt this many times. Consciously engaging with my feelings and my losses have helped me grow.

Bereavement is of course not confined to physical death, but physical death brings the loss home to us in a particular way. Depending on our personality and inner landscape, we may find it hard to express our grief. For whatever reason, we may feel blocked, numb or disassociated from deeply painful experiences that have shattered our hearts to bits. It may be the death of someone we loved deeply, the loss of a relationship or the ending of a life growing inside us. And even though it is part of being human to tense and close up when we are hurt or overwhelmed, over time the build-up of repressed energy can adversely affect us. In my therapeutic work I have observed at first-hand how a cathartic release accompanying a painful memory creates a shift in consciousness that moves the person on. The energetic release from uncovering and expressing the locked-in emotions frees up the heart energy which in turn can be mobilised in the service of our healing and soul growth.

The 'oer frought' Heart

At this time in our evolution as human beings, we have come to know the immense importance of the human heart in not just our physical but our emotional and mental well-being. With its vast electromagnetic field, the human heart can be classed as another brain, affecting all aspects of our being and consciousness and also mediating our connection with others and the universe. And although there is a tendency to cliché the 'connect to your heart' teachings of the 'wellness and mind-body-spirit' consciousness, making a mindful and felt connection with your heart is anything but a cliché. In a culture that values intellect and rationality at the expense of feeling and instinct, it can be a slow journey back to our hearts. Even though I would class myself as a deeply feeling woman, it has taken me some time to feel totally at home in both my physical body and my instinctual nature. And more importantly, to value my feelings as opposed to trying to conquer my emotions.

Jungian analyst and author Anne Baring describes the unique union that is our heart and our soul. She writes:

to respond to the quest for meaning in our individual lives, to find the pathway of connection to our deepest instincts, we need to listen to our heart, to feel its presence within us. The heart is the soul's organ of perception and plays a far greater role in our lives than we realize. The heart is the key to understanding how the instinct works, how powerful and all-pervasive and amazing it is.[31]

As a Jungian and spiritual therapist I know how the soul does not like to be split or compartmentalised and always seeks wholeness. The reality is that because of various factors, there are parts of us we have split or cut off, usually in reaction to painful or traumatic events; uncovering these 'lost' parts is vital to healing. A painful event and/or repressed feeling needs to be brought to consciousness, and the emotions expressed for true healing to happen. There is huge energy in blocked emotions that rationality alone cannot unblock. I remember saying to a journalist who was interviewing me about my work in childbirth that, *"It doesn't matter what happens to you, it matters rather how you feel about it."* I was referring to otherwise healthy women who nonetheless experienced the birth of their babies as traumatic and whose suffering was not recognised. I believe that *"what you don't feel you can't heal"*, and that it is important to both accept and express our emotions, most particularly when we are on a healing journey. Human emotions, messy as some may feel they are, in my view form part of the gateway to our spirituality. Our physical bodies, far from being a weakness we seek to overcome in the service of 'higher' consciousness, is the vessel of our soul. And it is often through the body that we access higher consciousness – a true embodied immanence. For me, healing comes from nature, our own and that of the world around us and our connection with spirit. There is great healing in nature where the cycles of life and death happen organically. It is well recognised that being in the natural world helps us connect with our own natures and can assist us in dealing with death and loss.

I am thinking all this as I walk by the sea on a particularly calm day. It had been a rough night with strong winds and angry seas. I had awoken several times to the angry howls of the wind and wondered if any damage would be caused. Miraculously, by morning, however, it was calm. I slip on my wellingtons and venture down the hill to the beach. The strand is strewn with seaweed; a thick band of slippery brown lines the high tide mark so that I have to negotiate the viscous mass as I approach the shoreline. There is not much beach left, the tide will be full shortly – I don't have much time. I pause to take a breath and watch as the sea edges closer and closer to nudge the grass embankment of the field above with its old and rickety barbed wire fencing. Gazing to the right where I know the small stones of the *Cillín* lie, almost buried now, it seems to me that the sea in her mourning, caresses and nurtures the land and her lost children, lulling them to sleep in their verdant earthy graves.

Landscape of Loss

hard to believe in that existence beyond graveyards, but you had a mouth pink peony cheeks a nose and eyes for laughter and pearly hands for reaching out and grasping the silver strings from heaven pulling you.
– Elizabeth Peavoy

Down the hill from my house and overlooking the beach lies a 'Cillín'. Wikipedia describes a *cillín* as:

a historic burial site in Ireland, primarily used for stillborn and unbaptized infants. These burial areas were also used for the recently deceased who were not allowed in consecrated churchyards, including the mentally disabled, suicides, beggars, executed criminals, and shipwreck victims.

And today, in an Ireland that has much changed, there still remains this landscape of loss, memorials to the 'un-mourned', especially in the West and where I live. Standing on these sacred and yet 'un-consecrated' sites, it feels to me as though the very body of mother earth weeps for the death of her children, thus marginalised and rejected by the Church. More, that the very soil holds inside it the disallowed and rejected grief of those who had to bury their loved ones, particularly their little babies, in unconsecrated ground.

As I navigate the grassy mounds of the "o'er frought heart" of the land, I have a keen felt sense that somehow I was guided to this particular area by my soul, perhaps because of my work. At the time, about thirty years ago, I was writing my first book, *Songs from the Womb,* and was very involved in uncovering and healing birth wounds and working with the pre- and perinatal level of experience. Healing mothers and babies was, I knew, part of my destiny. There was and still is a lot of healing needed both for the land of my birth and the families who lost babies and were prevented from burying their children the normal way, in consecrated ground. Many women (and their babies) have suffered greatly in a hitherto very closed Ireland dominated by a patriarchal and openly misogynistic Catholic Church. That suffering still exists on many levels. Women have stoically borne being forcibly and inhumanely separated from their babies, some incarcerated for most of their lives, their only sin, carrying and giving birth to a child out of wedlock.

It is not, however, the brief of this book to explore this area further.

Being acutely sensitive and connected to the land of my birth, before I came to live at this exact spot, I already sensed the loss in the landscape and knew somehow this is where I was meant to put down my roots – at least for a while. I was at that time living in London and my ex-husband and I were looking for a holiday cottage by the sea, near my home place.

The night before we were to meet the surveyor and engineer relating to the sale of the house and land we had agreed to buy, I had the following extraordinary experience. I woke suddenly during the night and in the dark saw the clear outline of a little girl. This 'vision' was accompanied by a sudden current of very cold air. It being a stormy night with strong winds, I thought at first it was my young daughter who was sleeping upstairs. Thinking she might have been disturbed or woken by the storm I called out to her and switched on my bedside light. There was no one there. Switching the light off, I lay in the darkness for some time, unable to fall back asleep, my heart beating fast. I intuitively knew this small being had come from the other side, a ghost if you will. I decided to converse with this little entity and asked her who she was and why she had come. There was a palpable sense of fear and loss in the air – it was still very cold. *"I fell down the well, they forgot about me,"* came the answer. I sent her love and told her to go to the light. After a while, when I felt she had left and the energy had changed, I went back to sleep. Next morning, at the appointed time, the engineer spread the land registry maps on the kitchen table and pointed out our land boundaries. On the map I noted a dot or x marking a particular spot in the front garden. *"What is that?"* I asked, pointing my finger to the spot. *"That is the well,"* he responded. I stared at him. *"Well?"* I queried. *"Yes, you have a well on your land,"* he replied. I could feel my hair standing on end! Seemingly the well had served many of the local people in the distant past when there was no mains water supply. Furthermore and unbeknownst to me at the time, the locals considered the well haunted. Then, some weeks later, when we moved in to the house, I discovered the remains of a small Cillín in the field directly below.

In my own spiritual journey as a woman and my healing life as a therapist, connecting with the Sacred Feminine and the Divine has come to me through nature and such deeply archetypal and corporeal experiences as pregnancy and childbirth. Here too, deep in my body came my first conscious, physical experience of death. As my dear late friend Elizabeth Peavoy writes above, on the death of her baby daughter at fourteen months, it is hard to believe in a life beyond graveyards, or in any transcendent existence that can bring comfort, when a life leaves before time. Losing a baby is a deeply embodied loss. Having lost two babies in the womb and suffered painful miscarriages with both, I know first-hand how it is to experience a death of 'what might have been' and to experience it in a deeply embodied visceral way. The loss of a baby in the womb has a special, poignantly painful energy. I still remember when I miscarried one of my babies at twelve gestational weeks and the way my body reacted with the crying (bleeding) of an empty womb, and even more devastatingly, how my breasts filled with milk, post 'birth'. They had been preparing to feed the new little life, bless them. And even though that was almost thirty years ago, the memory is fresh and vivid as I write this. It seemed to me then, as I sat weakly on my bed, breasts overflowing with milk that would never nourish, that I was filled with an excruciating physical paradox impossible to accept or contain. Something had gone wrong somewhere; carrying birth and death at the same time in my body defied the laws of nature and logic; it wasn't to be understood and could only be endured. I was reminded of this harrowing pain and paradox many years later after the death of a love relationship 'before time' when I wrote "A Death in Summer":

> Green and buzzing with life
> Summer had arrived barely seven days when you left me
> Instead of blooming into fullness, a slow death started in my heart
> As though autumn had come suddenly and devastatingly
> Interrupting summer and creating confusion
> So that the bud of love ceased growing
> And began

To turn inwards and wither before time

And it reminded me of another 'before time'
When the tiny seed inside me that had taken hold in the snow,
When spring came, turned back the other way towards death
When summer arrived that year, there was no baby
Only tears and an empty womb, heavy with new loss
When all around me was in full bloom
It seemed I was out of step somehow
A thin, sad figure in a time of flourishing life and long days

A Place of Tears: The Death Room

Even though death, as a transition, is part of the natural life cycle, most humans struggle with it. Grief and loss are part of life, and in the positive, may trigger in us a huge heart opening, especially if we engage fully with it. And for some, the strong heart and energetic connection between them and their departed loved ones can paradoxically open up a previously closed heart and trigger a spiritual awakening. As said, some losses are very hard to accept because they happen before time. But all losses carry with them gems from the heart that may serve as spiritual lessons, as well as triggering old unresolved or undigested traumas or emotional issues. I know all this, but I cannot escape the feeling of sadness that rises up in me as I head towards the healing room where I know several people await their treatment. This is the Death Room after all, a place of tears and loss.

First, however, I will visit the small meditation cave built into the side of the rock on the hill that leads down to the healing rooms. A tiny natural grotto, it was said to have once been an ancient monk's abode now serving as a meditation cave where soul pilgrims come to pray. It is late morning and the sun is high. When I arrive at the cave, I note, thankfully, there are no sandals or shoes by the entrance so I know I will be alone.

Slipping off my sandals, I bow my head and enter the small dark and slightly fusty hollow. Lit with several candles, the altar or 'pooja' lies at the far, narrowest end of the cave. Despite my small stature, I have to stoop as I approach. I relish the feel of the warm stone beneath my bare feet and the coolness of the air. Someone has placed flowers, some pictures and small oil-infused lamps by the Buddha statue. I sit in a lotus position on the small bench or ledge wedged into the wall and close my eyes. It is quiet and peaceful. After a while the grotto disappears and I am transported to a cave deep in the earth I recognise well. The familiar smell of damp earth fills my nostrils. I am with the earth Goddess Hecate whose torch and wheel betray her identity. As Goddess of the underworld, I know she has come to guide me on my own journey and my work in the death healing room where I will be helping people navigate their dark nights, heal their hearts and transition to the next phase of their spiritual journeys. After a while, I light the small tea light I have with me, and invoking the Goddess of the Crossroads' sacred energy and help, I utter a few words of prayer. Spending a few more minutes in quiet meditation, I open myself to whatever divine wisdom and guidance I am graced with. When I am done, I stoop my way out of the cave, slip on my sandals and head to the death healing room.

Before Time: Christina

That it will never come again
Is what makes life so sweet
– Emily Dickinson

Christina comes into the healing room. Tall and slight with large sad eyes, her clothes hang about her in a lost, forlorn way. She is still wearing her maternity clothes, I'm guessing. Her lovely face is etched in pain, and I cannot help the feeling of instantly wanting to hold her in my arms and comfort her. My heart stirs with compassion and I gently ask her to take a seat. Christina sits precariously on the edge of the chair facing me folding her long arms on her now hollow stomach. I notice her long delicate yet capable looking hands, resting now, but, I imagine, no stranger to tortuous wringing. She seems a lot older than the twenty-eight years indicated on her file. A stillbirth. The second one in two years. Each time she carried the child almost to term and then lost it. It was beyond bearable. This last time, just six weeks ago, with a renewed sense of hope that this time would be different, she had given birth to a beautiful baby girl. The baby had appeared healthy and vigorous in her womb and during labour, only to emerge, gasp once and die, her blue still limbs and perfect alabaster tiny body etched forever in her mother's heart. Since then, Christina had barely eaten, rarely slept and even more rarely spoke. Fearing for his wife, her anxious husband had pushed her to come to my healing room.

I sat opposite her and hoped that the big knot of compassion I could feel in my heart would somehow reach her. Knowing it was hard for her to speak about her loss, dammed up as she was in unshed tears and grief, I suggested she draw or paint. Christina nodded and approached the desk where art materials lay waiting. I watched her quietly as she chose a large white sheet of paper and several pots of paint and began. By the end of an hour Christina, still in silence, had covered four large sheets in deep dark red with streaks of black. I nodded and suggested we continue next week, and that if she felt like it, she could paint at home and bring the paintings in. Gently too, I urged her to write out her feelings, her own raw account of the pregnancy, birth, death and loss of her child.

"You don't even need to show it to me if you don't wish to, just write it for you – let your torn heart and bruised soul speak. Meanwhile, I'd like you to keep a diary, and to nurse yourself gently."
Christina looks at me and smiles briefly as she leaves clutching

her prescription; she seems lighter somehow. Her prescription for healing includes the following:

> We will meet regularly here, where Christina will have access to the healing tools she needs – paint, paper, pens – to facilitate her on her healing journey. An ongoing regular connection with me, her therapist, will ensure she has a quota of what she most needs at this time. Unconditional love, compassion and acceptance.

> At first it is hard for her to pray or meditate on her own but I do a healing and start each session with a chant and prayer invoking the Sacred Feminine and the nurturing healing energies of the mother Goddess. I invite her to join me.

> In time, and as Christina slowly unravels her tightly-closed heart and psyche, I will invite her to perform a healing, funeral ritual for her lost child. Knowing what form this ritual will take will unfold naturally from her, I leave it to her how she chooses to mourn.

> In time too, I will invite Christina to perform a healing ritual for herself as mother. Women who lose babies often unconsciously blame themselves and wonder what they did or did not do to cause the death of their foetus or child. And especially as this is her second stillbirth, Christina may turn against her body for failing to carry her child to term and give birth to a healthy live infant.

> Develop a daily ritual of nurturing herself. Until she is ready to do it for herself, I would encourage her husband or other person close to her to look after her by cooking nourishing foods, suggest she have a bath with essential oils by candlelight and have regular body treatments with a nurturing maternal figure. I would also encourage long walks in nature when possible.

> Daily affirmations such as: *"I honour myself as a mother," "I*

forgive myself, I love myself." This may be difficult at first, but with practice, it will happen organically.

Meditation and Forgiveness ritual. Although as her therapist I can provide unconditional love and acceptance, self-forgiveness is something I cannot. It must come from within as part of her self-healing. Here I suggest the ancient Hawaiian prayer of forgiveness. It is called Ho'oponopono. I include it below.

Praying/talking with her lost child. I have rarely met someone who does not have a sense of life beyond the physical, no matter how frail. It is always possible to connect with spirit. In the Buddhist view the spirit of the child may stay with you as long as you need it or until you release it. Talk to your spirit child. Letting go of the unlived whilst also understanding that life still goes on elsewhere on a different plane, undoubtedly helps the healing process.

Ho'oponopono: Prayer of Love and Forgiveness

Ho'oponopono is an ancient Hawaiian prayer of forgiveness comprising of four phrases used as a prayer or declaration. You say them usually during meditation or after quietening your mind and focusing on being in your heart. The phrases are used as a process for self-cleansing and letting go of the past. They are:

I am sorry.
Please forgive me.
Thank You.
I love you.

Saying the prayer continuously in your mind from a place of consciousness, and focusing on your heart, raises your vibration to one of love and forgiveness. The words create energy and intention to heal as well as a recognition that the pain, the loss you feel is in your life to be recognised and healed. *"Please forgive me"* states you recognise on some level that you have contributed to your pain because it exists energetically in your reality. Next, *"Thank you"* is an expression of gratitude. Feeling and expressing gratitude creates a very high vibration, and one we should cultivate daily in our lives. Giving gratitude is offering thanks to the Divine, which is in essence your true self. You are an aspect of God having a human experience; giving thanks recognises your true nature. When we practise gratitude our physical and energy body is filled with light and our vibration is raised. Next, *"I love you"* is a statement offered to the divine nature and reality of your being, and the divinity of the situation. Forgiveness is a very powerful way to cultivate bringing in the vibration of love. And no healing or soul work is done without love. This is a fundamental truth.

Letting Go: Joe

Unable are the loved to die,
For love is immortality.
– Emily Dickinson

Joe, a man in his sixties, comes into the room. For a well-built rather physically imposing man, Joe appears somehow crumpled and small. His handsome face is lined with sadness and his shoulders sag in the manner of overburdened coat hangers. I can't help noticing the missing buttons on his jacket and wonder if he is neglecting himself. He takes a seat opposite me and, unprompted, begins to talk. His wife of more than thirty years passed away three years ago. Cancer. At sixty-five he did not expect to find himself a widower. She was his heart he tells me, and when she died she took his heart with her. And although there is part of him that wants to live and even love again, he just cannot "connect" he tells me. Much of him feels numb. His friends and his daughters have all done their best to get him 'out there' and he even joined a dating site last year. He did meet some nice ladies, he says, but after a few weeks, things just petered out. He couldn't commit, he wasn't over his wife, according to Cathy, the last woman he dated, which lasted a couple of months. All this is background, however; what really troubles him are his dreams. *"Dreams?"* I ask, leaning forwards in my chair. *"What kind of dreams?"*

"Well, very busy and active, persistently sexual and increasingly salacious," Joe tells me, lowering his eyes as he does so. He seemed clearly embarrassed by both his dreams and his admission. Someone, an old friend who clearly worried about him, told him to come to me – that it might help to talk. That I might be able to help him clarify things and understand what was going on in his encumbered heart and overactive psyche.

"Do you feel you have let your late wife go?" I ask him gently.

Joe is not sure what I mean by letting go. He has mourned her, or thought he had, but deep down it is true that he does feel numb. He wants to think he can love again, or at the very least have a relationship, a life companion maybe. I ask him to tell me about his wife, about their life together. Later I will ask him what he wishes for his future. I let Joe talk without interruption for some time. Speaking about his late wife animates him, as though a light switches on inside him. Gradually, as he speaks and as the hour comes to a close, I see that Joe relaxes as he slowly unravels his overburdened heart. It is clear that Joe is conflicted. Guilt and desire jostle for space in his heart. He loved his wife and somehow feels disloyal or guilty about his natural desires to love and relate again. This is normal, but loyalty to a memory, to something that has passed and gone, blocks his natural life force so that like a dammed-up river, it must spill over. We will have to unblock the river and let it flow. As said, dissolution is not easy. Letting go is not easy.

"What about my dreams?" Joe interjects, as I tell him our time is almost over for today.

"We'll get to those next week, bring them with you," I answer.

"For now, I can tell you that creative, busy and sexual dreams are a sign of healing, a sign of life; your psyche wants to heal." Joe smiles for the first time in our session and I am glad of that. As he gets up to leave he seems taller somehow, as though something in him has uncrumpled, ever so slightly.

Sexual dreams are about a desire for connection and creating new life. Unlike the classical Freudian view, the Jungian interpretation of dreams is based on symbol, context and association, and the premise that our dreams have something valuable to tell us. Sex and sexuality in dreams is symbolic of union, of a creative desire for connection. An expression of the natural creative aspect of the psyche and of life that always seeks to renew itself. In this context, death is merely a transition, a stage of the eternal cycles of death and rebirth. When dreams come to us in the midst of a period of mourning, it is a good sign that we are ready for renewal, for new life.

I will ask Joe to record and bring his dreams to our sessions which will happen weekly for a time. His logical mind will no doubt enjoy the unravelling of seemingly meaningless symbolic images and give him some clarity on his own psychic process.

Talking therapy will help Joe unblock his complexed psyche and uncover some of the conflicting emotions that may be blocking him from truly moving on. Guilt at his desire to love again and move on from his late wife may be blocking his life force.

I also suggest a regular physical exercise regime. I do this quite deliberately because when we are employed by 'death' then we are not really in our bodies. Men do not have the natural archetypal pull to their bodies as we women do, who experience menses, pregnancy and childbirth. It is easier for men to disengage from their bodies and such initiatory experiences, and perhaps take flight in their 'minds'. Regular hikes or walks in nature can ground us in our bodies and therefore our emotions.

Most importantly, I will include breathing exercises to help Joe connect with his heart. These exercises are designed to gradually 'unthaw' and release the dammed-up emotions that result in the numbness Joe feels. I include a good method from the HeartMath Institute (www.heartmath.org) called the Quick Coherence® Technique. This or any other breathing practice and/or visualisation to bring awareness to the heart can be done as part of a meditation. I myself have found this exercise very helpful along with visualising Divine light flowing into the chakras and even the cells of the body. Adding heart releases love and healing energy, and harmonises our thoughts with our feelings.

To connect with his innate creativity, I invite Joe to pursue his favourite pastime or hobby. In Joe's case, it is woodwork. For anyone in mourning, anyone who feels lost by the pull of the past, pursuing an interest, an activity that gives him pleasure, that he enjoys, is very important. Working with his hands, as in carpentry or woodwork, will allow Joe to give form to his psyche, his innate life force. And it will ground him in the present.

To facilitate the letting go process, I encourage Joe to 'talk' and spiritually commune with his late wife, and likewise, as time goes forwards, to perform some kind of funeral ritual. I know that the form of such a ritual will emerge gradually, organically, as Joe heals.

Heart Connection: Quick Coherence® Technique

Focus your attention on the area of your heart, placing your hand on the centre of your chest. Heart-Focused Breathing involves the following. Imagine your breath is flowing in and out of that area, breathing slowly and gently in through your heart (to a count of five or six) and slowly and easily out through your heart (to the same count). Continue to breathe in and out in this way until your breathing feels smooth and balanced and has found a natural inner rhythm that feels good to you.

Continue to breathe through the area of your heart. As you do so, recall a positive image or feeling, a time or place where you felt happy and at peace with yourself, when you were doing something you enjoyed or felt love or compassion for a special person or animal, or aspect of nature, something that can bring a smile to your face as you recall it. Once you have connected with this feeling, sustain it while you continue to practise your Heart-Focused Breathing and Heart Feeling.

Heart Lock-In Technique

Hold the feeling of genuine love or care for someone or something in your life. Send this feeling of love and care towards yourself, extending it to the boundaries of the electromagnetic field that surrounds your body, then expand it to flow outwards towards others and to the wider world in the form of waves of energy. If you experience uncomfortable, anxious feelings, send love and compassion to those feelings. Befriending a negative feeling and sending compassion to it can release or dissolve the blockage. These exercises will gradually strengthen your conscious connection to your heart, build up resilience and the ability to be aware of subtle changes in its rhythm. I have found that over time, connecting in this way to your heart serves to both raise your vibration and anchor a sense of peace and love.

As I leave the healing room after my day's work, I see that the sun is going down. A dusky yet intense glow falls over the garden and the sea below, as though nature has turned on the lamp as it awaits the night. The lamp will be turned off as dawn arrives, next day. I am reminded of these words by Indian poet Tagore:

Death is not extinguishing the light; it is only putting out the lamp because the dawn has come.

Chapter Twelve

And Beyond

Do not look with fear on the changes or chances of this life; rather look at them with full faith that as they arise, God – whose you are – will deliver you out of them… either he will shield you from suffering or he will give you the unfailing strength to bear it.
– Francis de Sales

Although conceived previously, this book was written entirely during the coronavirus global pandemic. Writing during lockdown came easily and gratefully. The enforced confinement opened up a space for my imaginative heart out of which *The Soul & The Sea* was created. Although at times missing the company of my family and my grandchildren in particular, I relished the solitude that the lockdown facilitated. Being acutely aware of the blessings of living in nature and by the sea at a time when many others were having to confine in apartments in large cities, my spiritual practice and awareness intensified during this time. As a result, rather than contracting, my heart opened further. I experienced immense gratitude whilst at the same time great sorrow for the suffering of so many of my fellow souls affected by the pandemic. I became aware of the paradox of being alone and yet being connected to all. Despite the lack of physical relating imposed on us by the lockdown, love, relationship and soul bonds grew stronger in my heart together with a new listening and a new knowing of the certainty that we are all one. And that everything we think, feel and do affects others and the world in which we live.

At the same time, due to the many often uncomfortable and unsettling physical symptoms I was experiencing as part of a spiritual awakening and the planetary ascension process, writing became a welcomed balm. And a way to allow the new consciousness and lighter vibrational frequencies speak through me. As I wrote in my introduction, it is not that I have changed my initial teachings but that I have gone much further. Grounded in both archetypal and pre- and perinatal psychology, the foundations of human personality have not changed. We are undoubtedly informed by imprints from our early life and go on to animate our soul contract and life destiny. However, we are now part of a global evolutionary process in which more and more of us are awakening to a higher consciousness and evolving to a higher vibrational frequency. This means that what we have hitherto known becomes increasingly irrelevant to our future evolution and soul growth. Psychological insights are still useful and an essential part of coming to know ourselves, but we are fast approaching a time when this knowing is not enough. Developing our spiritual awareness, awakening to our divine natures and the knowledge that we have infinite possibility is vital to our evolution. Elevating our consciousness, attending to the way we live, to caring for each other, for animals and our mother the earth are all part of moving to a new age.

Ascension and COVID-19

Ascension is a process of aligning with higher consciousness. Planetary ascension provides that the earth (an organic being in its own right) is having its own spiritual experience by which it is moving from a dense low vibrating dimensional reality into a lighter, higher vibrating reality. As the earth moves through her ascension changing her electromagnetic field, all of us can be affected by the planetary changes and energetic shifts. Being part of the ascension process means your reality changes. You yourself change. Additionally, if you are an empath, you will feel the earth's shifts in your system. As these changes were manifesting in me, at first, I panicked. Having no reference point for the myriad of baffling physical symptoms I was experiencing,

I was lost. Sore throats and burning sensations in my chest that came and went, colds and respiratory symptoms that came to nothing, confused me. Fearful I might be getting the dreaded coronavirus, I would dose myself up with vitamins to boost my immune system. I would wake in the night with hot sweats and knew I had been dreaming. Or possibly downloading new vibrational frequencies and 'shakti' (cosmic energy) that would later pour into my work and writings. Medically, there was nothing wrong; I sensed that, but this didn't stop me initially from making futile calls to the doctor. When the symptoms were bad enough, I gravitated to spiritually-aware medical practitioners who worked with energy and quantum healing. In between I was aware of changing; I felt different. My old identity seemed to be crumbling. My intuitive knowing became sharper and clearer so that I came to trust what I saw, intuited and felt. At the same time as my inner 'sight' was becoming more clear, my outer vision gave me trouble. Sore dry eyes meant my contact lens wearing became less frequent. Suffering short bouts of unexplained nausea I found I could not tolerate foods I had hitherto enjoyed. My physicality felt 'unreal' at times and external reality appeared dreamlike, which I found a little alarming. My meditation cushion exerted a huge pull over me so that I often had to stop was I was doing to go within.

When I felt overwhelmed, I turned to prayer. During this time, I completed a 21-day Master Class with Sai Maa on quantum bio healing, designed to transform our physicality in preparation for the huge shift in consciousness happening on the planet. Through focused meditations and online instruction, Sai Maa worked directly with us on how to intentionally reprogram our cellular structure, guiding our cells towards health and longevity. I learnt that the ascension process can be hard on the physical body and that it is necessary to prepare for the increased light and vibrational frequency entering it. Eating alkaline foods, avoiding sugar and stimulants, meditation, sleep, exercise and rest are all part of this. Having completed the course, I certainly did experience a great lightness and could even 'see' increased light in my body. On the negative, however, at times I felt out of body and as though I was about to take off! I felt dizzy and disorientated for brief periods of time. However, adding a small amount of animal protein to my diet and various other grounding practices gradually normalised things. Being fortunate to live by the sea, my proximity to animals and nature also served to help me adjust to the transformational energies and to feel more grounded.

The Return of the Feminine

The future of the world depends on
The full restoration of the Sacred
Feminine in all its tenderness,
Passion, divine ferocity, and
Surrendered persistence
– Andrew Harvey

Many people all over the planet are experiencing a spiritual awakening, and their individual vibration or frequency is increasing. Their consciousness is expanding and their heart chakras are stirring. At a deep subliminal level, I sense we are moving through a new phase of life on our planet. I feel deeply that the pandemic, harrowing as it is, has come to teach us and that the world will never be the same again. From spiritual forecasters and sages, I understand that such a time had been foretold. A time of ascension and accelerated transition into a higher state of consciousness and ultimately a new age. A welcome return of the Sacred Feminine. We have been approaching the age of Aquarius for some time and it is not difficult to see that we are heading into an age characterised by a new consciousness, one guided by the heart, by compassion and humanitarianism. This is the return of the Sacred Feminine. It was time. We, along with the horrors we have inflicted on our mother the earth have become severely out of balance. We have felt ourselves invincible with our mighty armies of wealth, corporations, scientific advances and lots more. But the pandemic has shown us several things; one, there are no boundaries, the virus does not discriminate between countries, creeds or people. It doesn't care who or what you are or how much money, power or fame you have and where you come from. We are all interconnected. Second, it has revealed how powerless we are. Especially when instead of honouring the sacredness of all life, of love, of compassion and generosity, we have focused on the false gods of ego, money, supremacy and dominance.

The death of the old order, of patriarchy and a society dominated by fear, greed and dominance opens the way for the rebirth of the feminine principle and a society based on her values and the cyclical nature of existence. The goddess teaches a path of the heart, a path that all life is sacred, and that the intelligence that moves through the universe moves through each of us as well. This path honours the living energies of the earth and the spiritual beings behind the Cosmos. It honours the energetic connections between all peoples, animals and all earth creatures. We have learnt that we are all one, that what we do as individuals affects us all, and that 'no man is an island'. We have also learnt that we co-create reality and more than that, that by healing ourselves we heal the earth.

Author, clairvoyant and mystical teacher Tricia McCannon, in her beautiful book *Return of the Divine Sofia*, writes:

Long ago it was believed that the female was the natural mediator between the earth and sky, the physical and the spiritual realms. Thus we are about establishing a conscious partnership with the divine and learning to take responsibility for our own lives.

In the end this part is also about discovering the Divine spark within every creature and within every one of you. The path of the goddess teaches us that we are each responsible for our own spiritual development.[32]

To this end, our physical, mental and spiritual health is in our individual hands. The new age is very much about personal responsibility, a subject close to my heart and one I have been teaching this long while. That being said, despite an increased knowing of our ability to create our own healing and reality, there are times when we doubt. And doubting sends us on the path of fear. When our actions are dictated by fear rather than love, they are rarely kind or authentic, and take us away from the wisdom of the feminine with its heart-centred consciousness. Unshakable faith, trust and devotion to the Divine Mother or the Sacred Feminine is a life path. It can come upon us in mid or late life, or at any time and most particularly when an inner or outer event causes us to have an awakening and a change of heart. It is true to say that the path to enlightenment is up to each individual and through our own divinity.

I know of no better way to support our current evolution and spiritual growth than to spend time in nature, in self-discovery and contemplation. Prayer and mindful gratitude open up the portal to the divine. Earlier in the book I mentioned Gnosis, which can be described as a direct knowing or experience of God. From my own story and life experiences scattered throughout the fabric of the book, you will have noted times when I was graced with this direct knowing. All of us have the ability to connect with God, the Goddess or the divine through the portal of our hearts. That great fire of love beating in our chests. The Sacred Feminine is accessed through our hearts and not our heads, and as such comes from within. Just as healing is not a matter of will, but of surrender, acceptance and most of all, love. When our decisions are made from the heart, our relationships are dictated by kindness, tenderness and the strength that comes from fierce love and trust in divine order. True Gnosis is discovered through the eye of the heart and comes through direct experience or intuitive knowing. Most of us have to grow through this process as we are able to trust and come to realise that our egos are not in control of the vital flow of life.

Our Resilient Soul

I believe that the global pandemic has awakened not simply our compassion but our resilience. I feel that in many ways, we have been preparing for this time. The last few decades have seen a flowering of spiritual and wellness consciousness as we seek to become more whole and live more congruent lives. People are aware of and embracing higher consciousness. The learning of our powerlessness in the face of the virus allows us to surrender to a higher sovereignty. Now is the time to put into practice, to 'animate' the spiritual teachings we have learnt. About all being one, about inner empowerment, about conscious co-creation, about how we can together create a new world. Opening our crown (corona) chakras to our divine natures and the power of our spirit is crucial at this time.

From my own meditations, I know how light from the divine source enters directly through our crown chakras. Actively opening to and channelling this light gradually transforms and has the ability to heal us. And teach us how to be in a changing world. We are changing. During the past months, in the loneliness of the social distancing measures we have had to adopt, we have realised what is important. The truth of poet John Donne's words *"No man is an island"* resonates deeply within our hearts. We realise that love, compassion and our connection with each other, with nature and with our spiritual source are what matter most. I believe many of us feel this way, and that the pandemic has awakened humanity to love and to empathy and compassion, and the need to communicate from a higher consciousness and vibrational energy.

COVID-19 has further opened up the vast network of instantaneous communication available through the Internet. People of all ages have gratefully embraced such platforms as Zoom and Skype in a bid to keep connected during lockdown. Yoga, meditation, meetings and teachings moved online and showed us that energy and love are not confined to physicality and location. The power of worldwide prayer meetings via the Internet, world OMS, and all meditating together at the same time is creating a new healing, higher vibrational energy. All life breathes together; many know this, but it is not enough now just to 'know' with our minds. In the words of renowned psychotherapist Alexander Lowen, *"knowledge becomes understanding when it is coupled with feeling."* The ongoing global pandemic has resulted in untold pain and suffering which cannot fail but act as opener of the heart of humankind. There is a rise in community feeling and solidarity perhaps not seen since the world wars of the last century. I was immensely moved in the early months of the pandemic by images of the Italians singing in community from the windows and balconies of their locked-down country. Music, being the language of the Gods, kept many of us going during our confinement. In many ways the health crisis is bringing the world together. At time of writing we are nine months into the world pandemic but there is, hopefully, an end in sight. I believe that when we emerge from this crisis, the world will have shifted and changed forever.

'Titiksha'

This last January, just before the outbreak of the virus, I was fortunate to spend a healing two weeks at a yoga and meditation centre in India. A small hotel of merely a dozen rooms, mostly designed as small themed 'cottages' dotted around the gardens, mine was called 'Titiksha' (Forbearance in Sanskrit). On the wall in my room stood a plaque with a quote from the Bhagavad Gita:

The contacts between the senses and sense objects, O Arjuna, are the causes of heat and cold, pleasure and pain, Being transient, learn to withstand them.

With its message on forbearance, fortitude and patience, my temporary home seemed designed specifically for me! Not the most patient person, I consider these are soul qualities I am actively seeking to develop. Like many others, I sometimes grapple with my emotions and with understanding that, indeed, my feelings and my reactions are transient and will pass. As a deeply feeling woman I can get bogged down or overwhelmed at times and find it hard to simply 'detach' and go with the flow. I came to recognise and grapple with the wisdoms in the quote above in the course of working with my yogis and spiritual teachers during the retreat. After some practice, breathing techniques succeeded in helping me detach enough to understand that *I am not my body nor am I my emotions* – I am more than that. My essence, the light of who I am, is within me and I can connect with my true self through my breath. The spiritual teachings of yoga such as those designed to connect us to our life force or breath, allowing thoughts and feelings to come and go and not attaching undue importance to them, holds the key to achieving a form of emotional equilibrium. Our emotional state is generally dictated by the ego, an ego which is adept at creating the stories that we tell ourselves, such as, *"I am unloved and abandoned, I am not worthy, I'm not good enough."* As you will have read earlier in the book, our ego and our sense of separation from our divine selves is responsible for our suffering and inner turmoil.

That being said, detaching from or relegating our emotions to an inferior position might seem in conflict with the teachings of depth psychology. As a therapist I know that recognising and acknowledging one's emotions and engaging with the process of suffering is crucial to psychological and spiritual growth. Our sufferings often act as a call to consciousness. And I fiercely hold that there is no 'spiriting away' of emotional wounds. None. It takes the hard graft of soul work, being ruthlessly honest with oneself and a great deal of courage, faith and love to work through the barriers or obstacles we may be placing in front of our happiness and sense of well-being. So we need our feelings; the question is how to maintain emotional and mental equilibrium during such testing times. I've lived and worked long enough as a therapist to know that we can never eradicate suffering and that we will feel pain and hurt and loss and uncertainty, and that it is part of the human condition to have experiences that will unsettle our equilibrium and cause us pain. But I also know and trust that we are given the strength to deal with and endure our suffering, as noted by St. Francis de Sales in the quote above. The resilience of the human spirit in the face of adversity is amazing and wonderful.

From the Heart

Love is the bridge between you and everything.
– Rumi

Detaching from your feelings is not about taking you away from your heart. It is merely about helping you to maintain an equilibrium so that you do not become overwhelmed. For me, as I have already said, my feelings and my beautiful heart are actually the gateway to my spirituality. My humanness in all its flawed magnificent is the most precious gift I have. Feeling love in all my pores, in the cells of my body and in the great fire of my heart chakra is the fuel that propels me forwards in my life. And that sustains me during difficult times or when I am blind to the beauty and gift of life. And when I sleep, my dreams take over the task, rearranging my reality and bringing me further gifts. I know it is the voice of love in my soul that speaks to the poet and writer in me as I learn to navigate the vicissitudes of human life. As I write, a plaque with the words *"The heart that loves is always young"* beams its light from the wall above my computer. *The Soul & The Sea* has been written with great love and the excitement and joy that comes from being able to transmit spiritual teachings in my own unique way. Written entirely during the pandemic, I have been accompanied at all times by my great love the sea, which I can see out of my window, as I write. And I have been guided by the Divine Mother, the spirit of my ancestors and the Sacred Feminine as she speaks through them. My poem at the start of the book, *Spirit of The Sea*, articulates this connection and the direct line of energy and feminine wisdom passed to me and which I now seek to pass on to my own bloodline and all soul seekers.

It had been a wild day with howling winds and frequent cutting sleet showers that lash at the leathery backs of the cows grazing below my bedroom window. My room faces north and it is from the north that the wind blows most harshly. I feel for these earth creatures and wonder how they can survive the biting cold and freezing rain. Seeing them try to seek shelter by the inadequate hedges that line the north side of the field, I feel acutely for them and lament the fact there is nothing I can do. The neighbouring farmer does not possess a stable or barn. I salute them for their resilience and send them as much love as I can muster. Only this last spring they have given me the joy of seeing them give birth, anchoring in me a great fierce love for our mother earth and all her creatures and the ever renewing pulse of life.

It is now deep winter. As I write the final words of *The Soul & The Sea*, I wonder when next I will encounter the Goddess and where she will lead me and what she will have me write.

Bedding down in the depths and warmth of the earth I will sleep and dream of waking in the spring to a new world. My mother the sea will still call out on the tide that comes and goes and crashes to the shore. And we earth creatures will continue ebbing and flowing to our wholeness as we navigate our sacred human path.

For some she came in a dream. For others in words as clear as a bell: it is time, I am here. She may come in a whisper so loud she can deafen you or a shout so quiet you strain to hear. She may appear in the waves or the face of the moon, in a red goddess or a crow.

– Lucy H. Pearce

Endnotes

1. Thomas Cavalli, *Alchemical Psychology: Old Recipes for Living in a New World*

2. Oscar Wilde, *The Complete Letters of Oscar Wilde*

3. James Hillman, *Pink Madness*, Spring Audio, Inc., quoted in *Tragic Beauty* by Arlene Diane Landau

4. Benig Mauger, *Love in a Time of Broken Heart: Healing From Within*, p. 47

5. Arlene Diane Landau, *Tragic Beauty*, Foreword

6. B. Mauger, *Love in a Time of Broken Heart*, Ibid.

7. B. Mauger, *Love in a Time of Broken Heart*, p. 177

8. B. Mauger, *Love in a Time of Broken Heart*, p. 255

9. Rainer Maria Rilke, *Letters to a Young Poet*

10. Carl G. Jung, *Collected Works* 4, para 728

11. Benig Mauger, *Reclaiming Father: The Search for Wholeness in Men, Women and Children* (2004)

12. Emma Jung, *Animus and Anima*

13. Benig Mauger, *Songs from the Womb: Healing the Wounded Mother*, p. 50

14. B. Mauger, *Songs from the Womb*, p. 143

15. Clarissa Pinkola Estes, *Women Who Run with the Wolves*

16. B. Mauger, *Love in a Time of Broken Heart*, p. 269

17. RM Rilke, *Letters to a Young Poet*

18. C. Pinkola Estes, *Women Who Run with the Wolves*

19. RM Rilke, *Letters to a Young Poet*

20. CG Jung, *Collected Works* 11, para 391

21. Robert Bly, on Mothers, Fathers

22. B. Mauger, *Reclaiming Father: The Search for Wholeness in Men, Women and Children*

23. Ibid., p. 75

24. CG Jung, *Collected Works* 7, para 295

25. CG Jung, *Collected Works* 8, para 531

26. CG Jung, *Collected Works* 7, para 330
27. Caroline Myss, *Sacred Contracts*, p. 47
28. RM Rilke, *Letters to a Young Poet*, p. 98
29. B. Mauger, *Songs from the Womb*, p. 75
30. B. Mauger, *Songs from the Womb*, p. 42
31. Anne Baring, "The Importance of the Heart", from annebaring.com
32. Tricia McCannon, *Return of the Divine Sofia*, p. 65

About the Author

Benig Mauger is an internationally known Jungian psychotherapist, inspirational teacher, poet and workshop leader. Author of a number of critically acclaimed books, she is a frequent speaker at national and international events on psychological healing, spiritual wellness and how to live an empowered and soulful life. A pioneer in pre- and perinatal psychology, her groundbreaking book *Songs from the Womb* (1998) led to media exposure, seminars and workshops in the following years in the USA and Europe. Her books *Reclaiming Father* (2004) and *Love in a Time of Broken Heart* (2008) followed. Aside from her work as a speaker, teacher and author, Benig maintains a private practice as a therapist. Informed by her own spiritual journey, her recent work and writing is aimed at helping others learn how to heal from within. In a time of spiritual awakening and the return of the Sacred Feminine to our planet, Benig's work blends therapy and spirituality to provide tools for emotional and soul healing. She lives and works in Connemara, Ireland. Her work is featured on her website: www. benigmauger.com

Author's Note

Dear Reader. Thank you for purchasing *The Soul & The Sea*. My hope is that the book has offered insight and guidance into your own journey of profound healing and spiritual growth. Having chosen, by reading this book, to courageously enter the landscape of your soul and follow the journey to inner healing, know I am with you on this journey. If you have benefitted from this book, please feel free to add your review to online sites for feedback. I also encourage you to get in touch via my website: www.benigmauger.com to keep updated on future works, courses and workshops, and to subscribe to my newsletter: https://www.soul-connections.com/sign-up.
Blessings on your journey, Benig Mauger

O-BOOKS

SPIRITUALITY

O is a symbol of the world, of oneness and unity; this eye represents knowledge and insight. We publish titles on general spirituality and living a spiritual life. We aim to inform and help you on your own journey in this life.
If you have enjoyed this book, why not tell other readers by posting a review on your preferred book site?

Recent bestsellers from O-Books are:

Heart of Tantric Sex
Diana Richardson
Revealing Eastern secrets of deep love and intimacy to Western couples.
Paperback: 978-1-90381-637-0 ebook: 978-1-84694-637-0

Crystal Prescriptions
The A-Z guide to over 1,200 symptoms and their healing crystals
Judy Hall
The first in the popular series of eight books, this handy little guide is packed as tight as a pill-bottle with crystal remedies for ailments.
Paperback: 978-1-90504-740-6 ebook: 978-1-84694-629-5

Your Simple Path
Find Happiness in every step
Ian Tucker
A guide to helping us reconnect with what is really important in our lives.
Paperback: 978-1-78279-349-6 ebook: 978-1-78279-348-9

365 Days of Wisdom
Daily Messages To Inspire You Through The Year
Dadi Janki
Daily messages which cool the mind, warm the heart and guide you along your journey.
Paperback: 978-1-84694-863-3 ebook: 978-1-84694-864-0

Body of Wisdom
Women's Spiritual Power and How it Serves
Hilary Hart
Bringing together the dreams and experiences of women across the world with today's most visionary spiritual teachers.
Paperback: 978-1-78099-696-7 ebook: 978-1-78099-695-0

Dying to Be Free
From Enforced Secrecy to Near Death to True Transformation
Hannah Robinson
After an unexpected accident and near-death experience, Hannah Robinson found herself radically transforming her life, while a remarkable new insight altered her relationship with her father, a practising Catholic priest.
Paperback: 978-1-78535-254-6 ebook: 978-1-78535-255-3

The Ecology of the Soul
A Manual of Peace, Power and Personal Growth for Real People
in the Real World
Aidan Walker
Balance your own inner Ecology of the Soul to regain your
natural state of peace, power and wellbeing.
Paperback: 978-1-78279-850-7 ebook: 978-1-78279-849-1

Not I, Not other than I
The Life and Teachings of Russel Williams
Steve Taylor, Russel Williams
The miraculous life and inspiring teachings of one of the World's
greatest living Sages.
Paperback: 978-1-78279-729-6 ebook: 978-1-78279-728-9

On the Other Side of Love
A woman's unconventional journey towards wisdom
Muriel Maufroy
When life has lost all meaning, what do you do?
Paperback: 978-1-78535-281-2 ebook: 978-1-78535-282-9

Practicing A Course In Miracles
A translation of the Workbook in plain language, with
mentor's notes
Elizabeth A. Cronkhite
The practical second and third volumes of The Plain-Language
A Course In Miracles.
Paperback: 978-1-84694-403-1 ebook: 978-1-78099-072-9

Quantum Bliss

The Quantum Mechanics of Happiness, Abundance, and Health
George S. Mentz
Quantum Bliss is the breakthrough summary of success and
spirituality secrets that customers have been waiting for.
Paperback: 978-1-78535-203-4 ebook: 978-1-78535-204-1

The Upside Down Mountain

Mags MacKean
A must-read for anyone weary of chasing success and happiness
– one woman's inspirational journey swapping the uphill slog for
the downhill slope.
Paperback: 978-1-78535-171-6 ebook: 978-1-78535-172-3

Your Personal Tuning Fork

The Endocrine System
Deborah Bates
Discover your body's health secret, the endocrine system, and
'twang' your way to sustainable health!
Paperback: 978-1-84694-503-8 ebook: 978-1-78099-697-4

Readers of ebooks can buy or view any of these bestsellers by
clicking on the live link in the title. Most titles are published
in paperback and as an ebook. Paperbacks are available in
traditional bookshops. Both print and ebook formats are
available online.
Find more titles and sign up to our readers' newsletter at
http://www.johnhuntpublishing.com/mind-body-spirit
Follow us on Facebook at https://www.facebook.com/OBooks/
and Twitter at https://twitter.com/obooks